TRAINING

Gymnasium

Englisch – Fit für die Oberstufe

Rainer Jacob

STARK

Autor: Rainer Jacob hat durch seine Arbeit in der Lehrerfortbildung, der Lehrplankommission sowie als Studiendirektor und Englisch-Fachberater sehr viel praxisnahe Lehrerfahrung vorzuweisen.
Er veröffentlichte im STARK Verlag bereits zahlreiche Bücher und Unterrichtsbeiträge für das Fach Englisch.
Vom selben Autor sind im STARK Verlag u.a. die folgenden Titel erschienen:
- Abitur Training Englisch – Grammatikübungen
- Abitur Training Englisch – Themenwortschatz
- Abitur Wissen Englisch – Landeskunde Großbritannien
- Abitur Wissen Englisch – Landeskunde USA

Umschlagbild: © hxdbzxy / Shutterstock.com

www.stark-verlag.de
1. Auflage 1996

Inhalt

▶ Die grammatischen Strukturen, die mit diesem Icon gekennzeichnet sind, bereiten Schülerinnen und Schülern häufig Schwierigkeiten. Zu ihnen finden Sie leicht verständliche Lernvideos auf der Plattform „MyStark“. Darüber hinaus enthält die Plattform ein Video, das Ihnen Strategien zur Vokabelarbeit nahebringt. Zu „MyStark“ gelangen Sie über den Link und den Zugangscode auf der Umschlaginnenseite.

Audio-Dateien

Video-Dateien

Hinweis: Die Audio- und Video-Dateien können Sie über den Zugangscode freischalten, den Sie auf der Umschlaginnenseite finden.

Vorwort

Liebe Schülerin, lieber Schüler,

mit dem Übertritt in die Oberstufe kommt eine Reihe von neuen Herausforderungen auf Sie zu. Dieser Band unterstützt Sie dabei, die Hürden der Übergangsphase zu meistern und wesentliche Kompetenzen zu trainieren.

- **Reading:** Anhand von halboffenen und geschlossenen Aufgabentypen wie *multiple choice*, *true/false*-Aufgaben und *table completion* überprüfen Sie, ob Sie den Text verstanden haben.
- **Listening:** Die Aufgaben im Bereich Hörverstehen führen Sie schrittweise vom Erfassen der Kerninformationen des Textes zu einer intensiveren Auseinandersetzung mit Einzelaspekten. Achten Sie daher darauf, wie viele Hördurchgänge für die jeweilige Übungsaufgabe vorgesehen sind, und lesen Sie sich Vokabelangaben und Aufgaben vor dem ersten Anhören durch. Die Audio-Dateien können Sie auf der Plattform **„MyStark"** abrufen.
- **Mediation:** In diesem Kapitel finden Sie sowohl Aufgaben mit deutschem Ausgangstext, dessen Inhalt auf Englisch wiedergegeben werden soll, als auch englische Texte, die ins Deutsche gemittelt werden sollen.
- **Language in Use:** In den Kapiteln „Grammar" und „Vocabulary" können Sie sich noch einmal mit den Grammatikregeln, den Grundlagen der Wortbildung und der Verwendung von Wörtern im Kontext vertraut machen – oder Sie stellen Ihr Wissen gleich in den Übungsaufgaben unter Beweis.
  Zu grammatischen Strukturen, mit denen erfahrungsgemäß viele Schüler*innen Schwierigkeiten haben, gibt es zusätzlich Lernvideos.
- **Writing:** In diesem Kapitel können Sie ausgehend von ganz unterschiedlichen Impulsen (z. B. Bildern, Diagrammen, Cartoons, Werbeplakaten, Stellenanzeigen und Zitaten) Ihre Schreibkompetenz trainieren. Auch hier helfen Ihnen vorbereitende Aufgaben, Ideen zu sammeln.
- Am Ende des Buches finden Sie **Lösungsvorschläge** zu allen Aufgaben.

Zusätzlich können Sie viele Aufgaben **digital lösen**, was Ihren Lernprozess abwechslungsreich gestaltet. Auch zu den digitalen Aufgaben gelangen Sie über den Link und Ihren persönlichen Zugangscode (s. Umschlaginnenseite).

ActiveBook
Interaktives Training

Viel Erfolg bei der Arbeit mit diesem Buch!

Rainer Jacob

So arbeiten Sie mit dem „ActiveBook“:

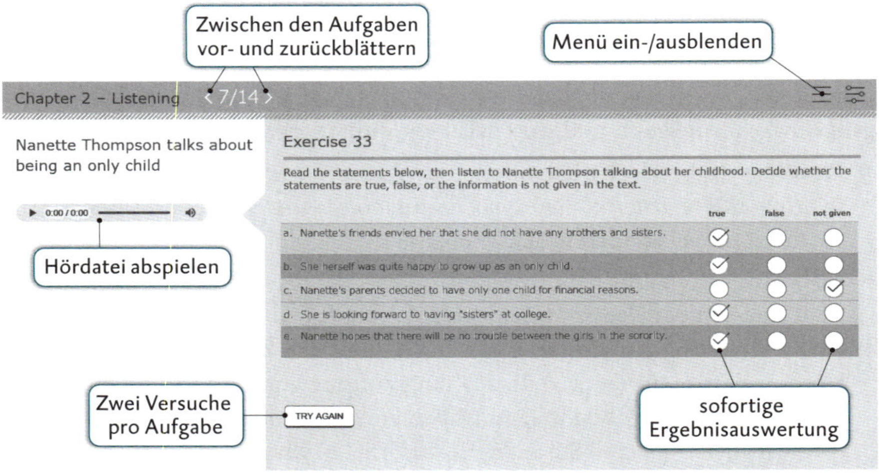

Tipps zur Bearbeitung von **Lückentexten** im „ActiveBook“:

- Achten Sie auf **richtige Groß- und Kleinschreibung**.
- Setzen Sie zwischen zwei Wörtern immer nur **ein Leerzeichen**.
- Erzeugen Sie den **Apostroph** (wie in *I'm*) durch gleichzeitiges Drücken der folgenden beiden Tasten: 

Reading

Non-Fictional Texts

Teenagers at work

Financial independence, work experience or simply meeting other people – part-time jobs have many advantages for teenagers nowadays.

1 ______________________________

In the UK and the US, young people aged 13 to 16 years are allowed to work not more than three hours on school days between 7 a.m. and 7 p.m. Whereas American teenagers are allowed to work no more than 18 hours a week altogether during the school year, teenagers in the UK can work 25 hours (13- to 14-year-olds) or even 35 hours (15- to 16-year-olds). However, there are special regulations for young people working as child actors or models or doing a paper round. While earning a bit of extra money is the reason why most teenagers choose to work as babysitters, car washers, grocery store stockers, waiters or tutors nowadays, in the past children were forced to work in order to support their families.

2 ______________________________

During the times of the Industrial Revolution in the 19th century, children were employed in mines and factories where they worked long hours in dangerous and filthy conditions. In some cases children of five and six years of age were forced to work from 13 to 16 hours a day. Before automatic machines were invented, the owners of mines and factories needed large numbers of cheap, unskilled labour. On the other hand, parents were so poor that they had to send their young children to work, just to make ends meet. Thus the children had no time to go to school, so they didn't learn how to read and write and later in life had to be satisfied with employment in menial jobs.

3 ______________________________

Work for minors was full of risks. Numerous accidents happened to children. Because of their young age they often didn't obey the safety rules, of which there were few anyway. Children often played in dangerous places. More than one got caught with his clothes in a turning wheel and died before the engine could be stopped. The luckier ones escaped with bad injuries, but were crippled for the rest of their lives.

4 ______________________________

By the middle of the 19th century child labour had produced an enormous number of illiterate, diseased and crippled children. Poor families had not got out of poverty – on the contrary, they had become poorer still. The famous writer Charles Dickens and the socialist Karl Marx brought the scandalous exploitation of children to the attention of a greater public. Due to constant pressure on politicians, the first significant British legislation against child labour was passed in 1878. It became illegal to employ children under the age of 10. Children between the ages of 10 and 14 were only allowed to work every second day or half days. For all children Saturday became a half holiday.

5 ______________________________

In spite of all the regulations aimed at protecting the health of children and securing their education the laws were not always effectively enforced. Children still worked hard and long hours not so much in mines and factories, but mostly in agriculture and in shops. There the laws could be broken quite easily because the children worked for their parents and nobody minded or complained.

6 ______________________________

Nowadays, teenagers working during school weeks are seen much more critically as a part-time job might have a severe impact on the end results, according to a study from the Institute for Social and Economic Research at the University of Essex. "Around a quarter of all 13- to 16-year-olds in England take some formal paid employment during school term time," said Dr Angus Holford, who conducted the study. "This can be a good thing – they earn their own money and can pick up useful skills, which might help them find full-time work in the future. However, they may spend that hard-earned money on less than useful things, or fall in with a different group of people. We did find that school children who worked became more likely to drink alcohol regularly, smoke or consume cannabis. It's inevitable that having a job gives teenagers less time to study. What concerns me is how it causes teenagers to lose sight of the importance of their education for their longer-term opportunities."

(682 words)

Source: Paragraphs 1–5: © Rainer Jacob; Paragraph 6: Tracy McVeigh, in: The Observer, *28th March 2015 (adapted)*

Annotations

(to) do a paper round (ll. 6/7): (to) deliver newspapers regularly; filthy (l. 13): dirty; labour (l. 16): workers; (to) make ends meet (l. 17): *über die Runden kommen*;

menial (l. 19): unskilled; (to) enforce a law (l. 36): (to) make sure that this law is obeyed; severe (l. 42): very bad; (to) fall in with sb (l. 49): (to) join sb; inevitable (l. 51): sure to happen

Basics

Lesestrategien

Je nach Leseziel können ganz unterschiedliche Vorgehensweisen eingesetzt werden, um Informationen aus Texten zu erschließen.

- ***Skimming:*** Mit dieser Lesestrategie kann schnell festgestellt werden, worum es in dem Text grob geht. Oft eignet sich diese Methode, um Textabschnitten die richtige Überschrift zuordnen zu können oder eine Textzusammenfassung zu erstellen. Dazu lesen Sie den Text „quer", d. h. Sie entnehmen nur die wichtigsten Informationen. (Beispiel: siehe Aufgabe 1)
- ***Scanning:*** Wenn Sie z. B. einzuschätzen sollen, ob Aussagen wahr oder falsch sind, benötigen Sie nur bestimmte Informationen. Durchkämmen Sie den Text also nach Stichworten, die vielleicht schon in dem Satz gegeben sind, dessen Wahrheitsgehalt Sie überprüfen sollen. Hier geht es darum, an spezifische Informationen zu gelangen. Diese „key words" können bspw. Ländernamen, Namen von Personen oder Zahlenangaben sein. (Beispiel: siehe Aufgabe 2)
- ***Reading for detailed information:*** Das Ziel des Lesevorgangs kann es z. B. sein, eine Tabelle mit Informationen aus dem Text zu vervollständigen oder eine Situations- bzw. Charakteranalyse vorzunehmen. Dann müssen Sie einen Text(-abschnitt) genau lesen und auf jedes Wort achten. Dies ist vor allem wichtig, wenn Informationen zwischen den Zeilen gegeben werden, also von Ihnen aus dem Sinnzusammenhang interpretiert werden müssen. (Beispiel: siehe Aufgabe 3)

1 Read the text "Teenagers at work" carefully, then choose the correct heading (A–H) for each paragraph (1–6). There are two more headings than you need. Write the corresponding paragraph number in the first column on the left.

	A	Still more protection needed for working youngsters
	B	Violation of laws against child labour
	C	Current working regulations for young people
	D	Jobs prevent teenage education
	E	Child labour in poorer countries
	F	Long-term consequences of child labour in the past
	G	Health hazards for child labourers
	H	Efforts for the protection of working children

2 Read the text again and decide whether the statements are true or false. Mark the correct box with a cross (✗).
Correct the statements that are wrong in a few words.

	true	false
a) In the United States young people of 13 to 16 years of age may work up to three hours every day.	☐	☐
b) Very often children work to become more financially independent.	☐	☐
c) In the past, even very young children had to work to contribute to the family income.	☐	☐
d) In the 19th century many working children were unable to read or write.	☐	☐
e) Many accidents happened in the factories because children were not told about how dangerous machines could be.	☐	☐
f) Charles Dickens and Karl Marx were two politicians who tried to improve the situation of working children.	☐	☐
g) The new laws which limited the hours children were allowed to work were not respected by farmers and shop owners.	☐	☐
h) Teenagers who work part-time learn to take care of themselves better.	☐	☐

3 Find information on the following topics in the text.

	Working young people in the past	Working young people at present
jobs		
age		
working hours		
hazards		
measures taken or suggested		

The darker side of fame

Very often tyrannical managers, demanding audiences and unscrupulous businessmen expect the superstar to continue playing a role and living up to the image they have given him. What they do not consider are the feelings of the human being behind the glittering façade.

Case 1: Kurt Cobain

He was 27. With his band Nirvana he had sold millions of CDs and had become one of the most successful rock heroes to millions. In April 1994 Kurt Cobain took a shotgun and killed himself. On receiving the news of her son's suicide Kurt's mother said, "Now he's gone and joined that stupid club. I told him not to join that stupid club". What she meant was that "stupid club" of young rock stars whose lives had ended before they had reached the age of 30. Rock legends like Jimmy Hendrix, Janis Joplin and Jim Morrison destroyed themselves with drug and alcohol abuse. Kurt Cobain, too, was a heroin user.

Kurt had a very unhappy childhood. The divorce of his parents when he was eight hurt him deeply. His mother and her new husband constantly argued and even threatened to kill each other. Kurt wanted to escape from this unpleasant world of the grown-ups and started taking drugs. The music of the punk groups he listened to also expressed his contempt of adult society. So after trying his luck at several jobs he formed a band of his own with two friends. They called it Nirvana and produced their first album, *Bleach*, in 1988.

Their second album *Nevermind* (1991) reached the top of the charts in no time, selling over 10 million copies. Touring the USA and Europe brought money, fame – and also stress and more drug-taking. Kurt and his band became rich by telling the world how much they hated the establishment. They had started out as rebels against society, but the ironic and tragic thing happened: the outsiders, the outlaws became wealthy and famous. What followed was an identity crisis which eventually led Kurt Cobain to end his life.

Annotations

contempt (l. 18): feeling of angry disrespect, hatred

Case 2: Michael Jackson

Singer, dancer and songwriter Michael Jackson was the darling of the media but became the target of world-wide criticism, scorn and indignation when a boy of 13 accused him of sexual abuse. Born on August 29, 1958, in Indiana, young Michael made his show debut at the age of five as the youngest member of his brothers' pop group, the Jackson Five. Michael, a very talented dancer and singer, soon became the favourite with the audience. However, behind the scene things were different: Michael's tyrannical father frequently told him off and beat him. In the end, Michael paid for his success with the loss of his childhood.

Aged 13, Michael left the family group and started an extremely successful solo career. His albums and the videos of his songs belong to the most popular and best-selling recordings ever made. Michael Jackson's dancing style, his very special way of dressing and his physical appearance made him a spectacular event on the stage. Because of his eccentric lifestyle, the "King of Pop" was a frequent subject of the gossip columns in the trashy weeklies. His skin became whiter and whiter and there were rumours that plastic surgery had not only changed his face but also his character and personality.

Michael sought peace on his ranch "Neverland" – named after an island in the children's book *Peter Pan*, where children never have to grow up. There he surrounded himself with young boys. He said he himself had been deprived of a normal childhood and wanted to create a paradise for as many children as possible. The stress of being a superstar eventually took its toll. Jackson became addicted to drugs and tranquillisers. On June 25, 2009, he died in Los Angeles.

Annotations

target (l. 2): victim, aim; trashy (l. 19): cheap, rubbishy; (to) deprive sb of sth (l. 24): (to) take sth away from sb, not allow sb to have sth; (to) take its toll (l. 26): (to) have a very bad effect; tranquilliser (l. 27): a drug taken to calm the nerves and reduce tension

Case 3: Amy Winehouse

Amy Winehouse, born in 1983, had been a rebel since early childhood and frequently got into trouble at school. Her parents divorced when she was nine years old. She had to change schools several times and got her first tattoo and a pierced nose at the age of 14. After graduation, she attended the famous BRIT School, a school for performing arts and technology in London, but left it after only one year. Her first album, *Frank*, received a lot of attention in Britain when it was released in 2003, but was not recognised on an international level at that time. After the end of a very painful and destructive marriage, Amy's second album, *Back to Black*, made her both famous and rich in 2007. Her deep voice and her very special style of music, a mix of soul, rhythm and blues, jazz and reggae made her songs unique and extremely popular. Amy's beehive hairstyle and her way of dressing resulted in a comeback of the fashion of the 1960s.

However, the singer, who started drug trafficking during her marriage, struggled hard to fight her addiction and in the end was not able to quit drinking altogether.

Various attempts to stay clean failed. The release of her third album and a tour throughout Europe had to be cancelled after she appeared completely drunk on stage and was unable to perform. Amy Winehouse died of alcohol poisoning in 2011 at the age of 27. *(832 words)*

Source: © Rainer Jacob

Annotations

destructive (l. 10): upsetting, hurtful, causing a lot of pain; (to) traffick (l. 20): (to) buy or sell sth illegally

4 Read the text "The darker side of fame" carefully.
Then choose the correct solution and mark it with a cross (✗).

a) Kurt Cobain's mother …
- [ ] did not want her son to start a career as a musician.
- [ ] was surprised when she learned that Kurt had killed himself.
- [ ] was always afraid that Kurt might commit suicide in the end.
- [ ] had no idea of the stress her son was under.

b) Kurt Cobain became involved with drugs because …
- [ ] it was the fashion of the time.
- [ ] he was unhappy with his life.
- [ ] they helped him make better music.
- [ ] that was his way of rebelling against his parents.

c) With their music Cobain and his band …
- [ ] expressed their protest against the adult world.
- [ ] showed their fans visions of a better future.
- [ ] wanted to earn as much money as possible.
- [ ] intended to create a new style of music.

d) Michael Jackson's career came to a halt when …
- [ ] he started taking drugs.
- [ ] the tyrannical behaviour of his father increased.
- [ ] the Jackson Five broke up.
- [ ] rumours of sexual abuse were made public.

e) Michael Jackson earned particular fame because of his …
- [ ] strange appearance.
- [ ] talents as a dancer and singer.
- [ ] frequent appearance in the media.
- [ ] special lifestyle.

f) It took Amy Winehouse some time to become famous because …
- ☐ she was heavily addicted to drugs and could not perform well.
- ☐ her first album was only noticed on a national level.
- ☐ she had a very difficult personality.
- ☐ she was not a mainstream singer.

g) What made Amy Winehouse's music special was …
- ☐ her voice, which frequently cracked.
- ☐ her extraordinary performances on stage.
- ☐ the combination of different styles of music.
- ☐ the topics she sang about.

5 Match the corresponding parts of these sentences.

1 Many famous people died early …
2 Kurt Cobain and his band were successful …
3 Michael Jackson bought "Neverland" …
4 Music companies, managers and fans play a decisive role …
5 Many celebrities lose control of their lives …
6 Amy Winehouse's look created a new trend …

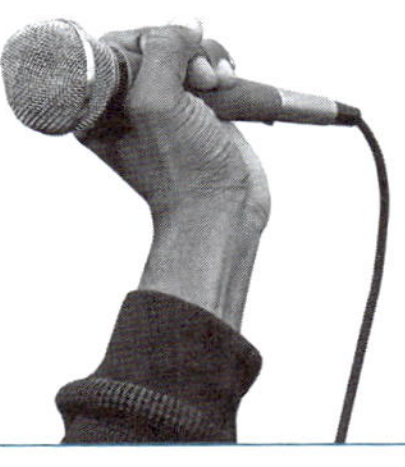

A as they increase the pressure on the stars.
B because he wanted to make up for the loss of his own childhood.
C because fans started to dress in the fashion of the 1960s.
D because of their destructive lifestyle.
E because they expressed the feelings of their generation.
F because they cannot cope with the stress which comes with fame.

1	2	3	4	5	6

Basics

Offene Aufgabenstellungen zum Inhalt des Textes

Was wird verlangt?

Hierbei handelt es sich um „textinterne" Aufgaben, d. h. die Antworten sind meist vollständig im vorliegenden Text zu finden. Bei der Beantwortung sollen Sie zeigen, dass Sie den Text insgesamt verstanden haben und in der Fremdsprache eine sinnvolle Antwort geben können. Sie stehen vor einer doppelten Aufgabe:

- Finden Sie im englischen Text die Stelle, die die Aufgabenstellung beantwortet.
- Verfassen Sie eine Lösung, die die wesentlichen Inhalte in eigenen Worten ausdrückt.

Wie gehen Sie vor?

Suchen Sie zuerst im Originaltext Informationen, die Ihnen helfen, die Aufgabenstellung zu bearbeiten. Markieren Sie diese Stellen im Text. Versuchen Sie, die gefundenen Inhalte mit eigenen Worten wiederzugeben.

Beachten Sie besonders folgende Aspekte:

- Vermeiden Sie Wiederholungen („and then …, and then …") oder abgegriffene Formulierungen, z. B. Verben wie „be", „have", „get" oder Adjektive wie „good", „bad", „nice".
- Vermeiden Sie unklare Bezüge und zu allgemeine Formulierungen („they", „it", etc.).
- Achten Sie darauf, dass Sie bei einer Zeitstufe bleiben und nicht zwischen verschiedenen Zeiten hin- und herwechseln. Orientieren Sie sich an der Zeit, die in der Aufgabenstellung verwendet wird.

6 Read the text "The darker side of fame" and complete the following tasks.

a) Give reasons why people usually do not consider the negative consequences of being famous.

____

____

____

____

b) Explain what Kurt Cobain's mother meant when she told her son "not to join that stupid club" (Case 1, l. 7).

____

____

____

____

c) Relate how Kurt Cobain's identity crisis was brought about.

d) Sum up the developments that led to Michael Jackson's downfall.

e) Describe how Amy Winehouse changed after the release of her first album.

f) Find parallels in the lives of Kurt Cobain and Amy Winehouse.

Gap year "voluntourists"

"Voluntourism" has come in for plenty of criticism in recent years, but the stereotype of volunteers as well-meaning but incompetent students on gap years may need a rethink after a new report highlighted the "unique contribution" made by them in the fight to end poverty.

The researchers, who spent two years speaking to more than 3,700 participants from four different countries, were from Voluntary Service Overseas (VSO) and the Institute for Development Studies (IDS). They found that volunteers make a valuable, yet often understated, impact on sustainable development, and that they can be an effective means of reaching poor and vulnerable communities while also giving them access to valuable public services. In Mozambique, for example, the number of Aids patients receiving home-based care provided by volunteers rose from 17,790 to just under 100,000 [in only four years].

Among the report's central findings was that having volunteers embedded in the local community they are supposed to be supporting helps promote trust and effective partnerships. Volunteers were also found to be engaging in meaningful projects to share their skills with local workers and help alleviate their workload, while simultaneously fostering a new spirit of altruism within the communities they worked in.

However, it was not all good news. According to the report, problems occur when the relationship between the community and volunteers becomes too one-way, with community members dependent on volunteers for skills and NGOs reluctant to share their knowledge.

[...] There was also evidence of volunteers being used to plug gaps in essential public services, with local workforces blighted by poor pay, lack of training and absenteeism. [...]

So does this mean that all the dire warnings about the impact of so called "voluntourism" schemes on developing countries are overstated? Not according to Mark Watson, executive director of the charity Tourism Concern.

"There's a difference between voluntourism and doctors going to help in a developing country," he argues. "One thing Africa is not short of is unskilled labour, so western teenagers going over there to help can end up taking away jobs from local people. In our experience, genuine volunteering organisations will sell these trips as ways of self-improvement for young people, rather than making claims about them aiding development."

Katie Turner [of VSO] argues that voluntourism is not a bad thing in and of itself. “This was a learning piece for us. We’ve used it so we can understand how volunteers can be used more effectively, and look at how we can support them better,” she says. “We don’t believe that all voluntourism is bad. It depends on the impact it has on the ground. From our point of view, if it’s purely a case of volunteering for the sake of the volunteer, that’s not truly volunteering. It has to be about the impact of the work on the ground.”

(470 words)

Source: Joe Sandler Clarke, on: www.theguardian.com, 4th November 2015

Annotations

voluntourist (heading): blend of volunteer and tourist; impact (ll. 16/17): effect, influence; sustainable (l. 17): *tragfähig, nachhaltig*; NGO (l. 45): non-governmental organisation; (to) plug gaps (l. 48): (to) provide something that is lacking in a particular situation; (to) blight (l. 50): (to) harm, destroy; absenteeism (l. 51): regularly staying away from school or work; dire warnings (ll. 52/53): warnings of negative consequences

Blogger 1

I agree that voluntourism can be positive, contributing to the development of poorer people in disadvantaged regions of our planet. However, I believe that through their work volunteers take away jobs from local people. Therefore, in my view, it would be better if volunteers donated the money they spend on airfare and expenses to finance a project hiring local workers.

Blogger 2

It is totally wrong to maintain that volunteers take jobs away from locals. Many of the projects they work on wouldn’t even exist if volunteers weren’t there. Instead of slating well-meaning young people and their projects critics should encourage them in their efforts and see something positive in voluntourism.

Annotation

Blogger 2: (to) slate sb (l. 3): (to) criticise sb harshly

7 Read the newspaper article "Gap year 'voluntourists'" and decide which of the alternatives provided is correct. Mark the correct version with a cross (**✗**).

The article …

- ☐ provides information on possibilities for young people working abroad.
- ☐ summarises the findings of a study on voluntourism.
- ☐ warns about the negative effects of development aid.
- ☐ criticises the work of well-meaning volunteers in developing countries.

8 Read the text again carefully and complete the sentences with a maximum of five words. Use your own words as far as possible.

a) It has been held against "voluntourists" that they …

____

____

b) However, a new study found that the work of volunteers stimulates …

____

____

c) Thanks to young volunteers in Mozambique, an increasing number of AIDS patients were …

____

____

d) Local communities as a whole benefit from the volunteers' …

____

____

e) One negative effect of "voluntourism" is that locals …

____

____

f) To assess whether "voluntourism" is a real help for developing countries, one has to …

____

____

9 Complete the mind map below on the pros and cons of doing a gap year or volunteering. Use your own words and also refer to the bloggers' comments.

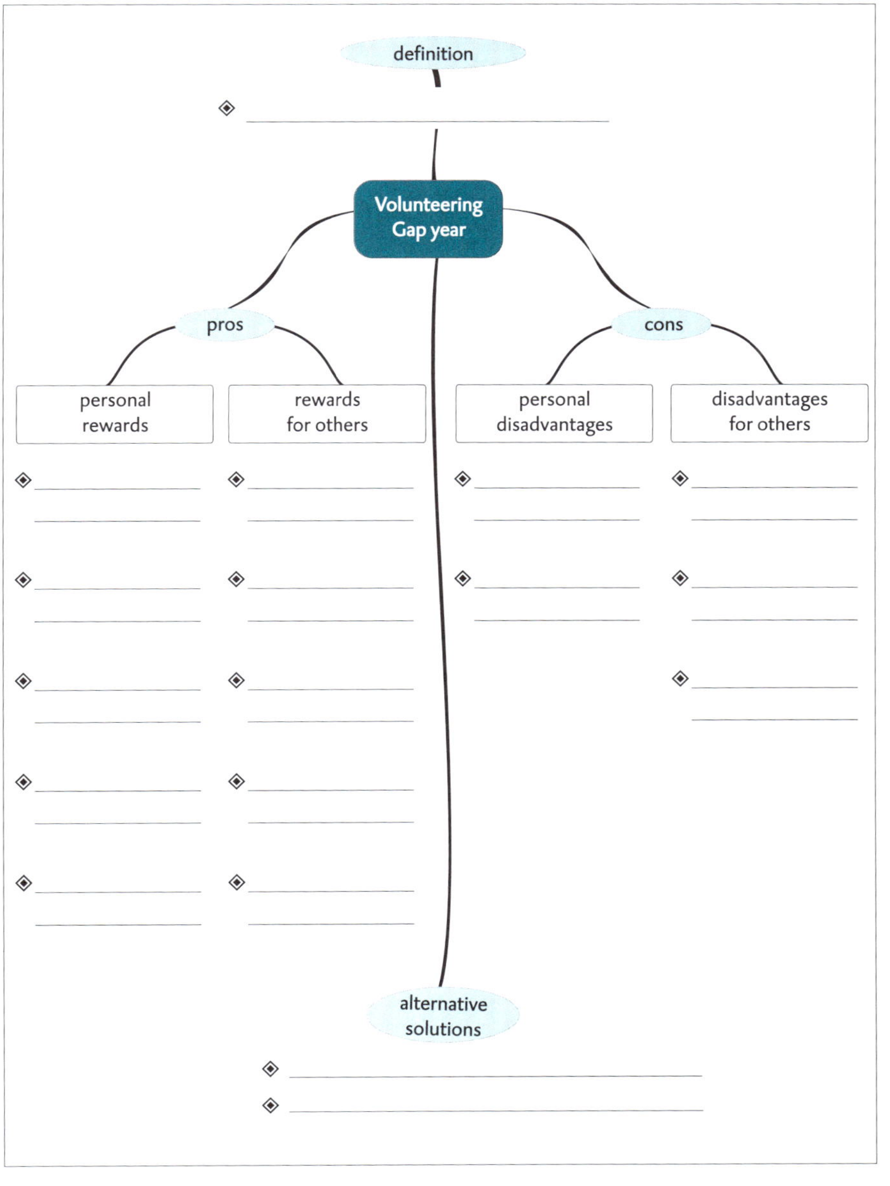

Fictional Texts

Micro stories

Latest Entry by Michael Lawrie

Eleanor would die within the hour.
She had drunk the bottle of whisky, swallowed more than enough of the pills and prepared a beautifully written final posting for her Livejournal. She'd show them, they'd be sorry now. She'd really done it!
She clicked "Upload" and the computer told her to try again in two hours.

From: http://uknet.com/gallery2/55-Fiction/latest_entry.jpg.html *(55 words)*

Survival of the Fittest by Michael Lawrie

The New Humans gathered on the remote mountain range. Each represented the pinnacle of evolution, far removed from the brutality that was Mankind.
The old race would be gone in a month. The virus was selective, deadly, ruthless, and carefully designed not to affect the New Humans.
"They'd have killed us," mused one …
"Wouldn't they?"

From: http://uknet.com/gallery2/55-Fiction/survival.jpg.html *(56 words)*

Meeting People by Alistair Reed

"So what do you do?" He said
"I'm in TV, editing" She said
"How did you manage that?"
"I don't know really. It was my first application."
"First one? No way."
"You? How many applications? Actually what do you do?"
Picks up a tray on a table behind him.
"Canapé?"

From: http://www.tangents.co.uk/50words/stories/136.html *(50 words)*

Annotations

Survival of the Fittest: pinnacle (l. 2): highest form; ruthless (ll. 3/4): cruel, without mercy;
Meeting People: canapé (l. 8): small piece of bread with cheese, meat etc. on top (party food)

10 For each story, choose one image that illustrates it best.

Micro Story	Latest Entry	Survival of the Fittest	Meeting People
Picture			

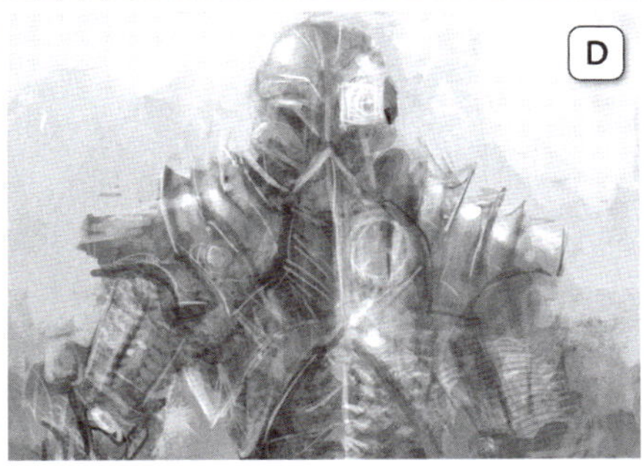

11 Find two alternative headlines for each story.

Micro Story	Latest Entry	Survival of the Fittest	Meeting People
Alternative Headline			

12 Read the micro stories again. Then mark the correct solution with a cross (✗).

a) The atmosphere in "Latest Entry" can be described as …
- ☐ pitiful and emotional.
- ☐ menacing and hostile.
- ☐ relaxed and exciting.

b) The setting of "Survival of the Fittest" can be referred to as …
- ☐ lonely and cold.
- ☐ spacious and vast.
- ☐ warm and welcoming.

c) The characters in "Meeting People" seem to be …
- ☐ depressed and sad.
- ☐ majestic and mighty.
- ☐ chatty and friendly.

13 Read the interpretations of two of the three stories and fill in the gaps with the correct form of one of the following words.

(to) blame • brutal • designer • (to) extinguish • (to) get rid • (to) leave • message • (to) replace • revenge • suicide • technical • triumph

The micro story "Latest Entry" is about a young woman who has prepared her ______________. However, before ______________ for good, she wants to send a ______________ to the world to let everyone know how badly she was treated and to take ______________. It is her wish to let everybody know who is to ______________ for what she had to do. However, because of a ______________ fault, the final posting cannot be distributed. Thus, sadly, nobody will ever get to know her side of the story.

"Survival of the Fittest" can be referred to as an illustration of Darwin's law: A new race, "the New Humans", is about to ______________ of Mankind, the old race. Within a month a new deadly virus will ______________ the old breed and make room for a new superior species. The New Humans seem to be the ______________ of the lethal disease in order to create a new world. The means applied by the New Humans to reach their aim are as ______________ as the ones used by Mankind. According to Darwin's theory of natural selection, the ______________ of the new race is not the end of evolution, however. Sooner or later, the new rulers will be ______________ by a more sophisticated species.

Eveline

Part 1

She had hard work to keep the house together and to see that the two young children who had been left to her charge went to school regularly and got their meals regularly. It was hard work – a hard life – but now that she was about to leave it she did not find it a wholly undesirable life.

She was about to explore another life with Frank. Frank was very kind, manly, open-hearted. She was to go away with him by the night-boat to be his wife and to live with him in Buenos Ayres, where he had a home waiting for her. How well she remembered the first time she had seen him; he was lodging in a house on the main road where she used to visit. It seemed a few weeks ago. He was standing at the gate, his peaked cap pushed back on his head and his hair tumbled forward over a face of bronze. Then they had come to know each other. He used to meet her outside the Stores every evening and see her home. He took her to see *The Bohemian Girl* and she felt elated as she sat in an unaccustomed part of the theatre with him. He was awfully fond of music and sang a little. People knew that they were courting, and, when he sang about the lass that loves a sailor, she always felt pleasantly confused. [...] First of all it had been an excitement for her to have a fellow and then she had begun to like him. [...] Of course, her father had found out the affair and had forbidden her to have anything to say to him. [...]

One day he had quarrelled with Frank, and after that she had to meet her lover secretly.

The evening deepened in the avenue. [...] Her father was becoming old lately, she noticed; he would miss her. Sometimes he could be very nice. Not long before, when she had been laid up for a day, he had read her out a ghost story and made toast for her at the fire. Another day, when their mother was alive, they had all gone for a picnic to the Hill of Howth. She remembered her father putting on her mother's bonnet to make the children laugh.

Her time was running out, but she continued to sit by the window [...]. Down far in the avenue she could hear a street organ playing. She knew the air. Strange that it should come that very night to remind her of the promise to her mother, her promise to keep the home together as long as she could. [...]

She stood up in a sudden impulse of terror. Escape! She must escape! Frank would save her. He would give her life, perhaps love, too. But she wanted to live. Why should she be unhappy? She had a right to happiness. [...] *(486 words)*

Source: Joyce, James: "Eveline". In: Joyce, James: Dubliners. *London: Grant Richards Ltd. 1914*

Annotations

peaked (l. 10): pointed; (to) tumble (l. 11): (to) fall; *The Bohemian Girl* (l. 13): an opera by the Irish composer Michael W. Balfe (1843); elated (l. 13): extremely happy and excited; unaccustomed (ll. 13/14): not used to sth; (to) be courting (l. 15): (to) have a romantic relationship; bonnet (l. 27): an old-fashioned women's hat that is tied under the chin; air (l. 29): melody, tune

Part 2

She stood among the swaying crowd in the station at the North Wall. He held her hand and she knew that he was speaking to her, saying something about the passage over and over again. The station was full of soldiers with brown baggages. [...] She answered nothing. She felt her cheek pale and cold and, out of a maze of distress, she prayed to God to direct her, to show her what was her duty. The boat blew a long mournful whistle into the mist. If she went, to-morrow she would be on the sea with Frank, steaming towards Buenos Ayres. Their passage had been booked. Could she still draw back after all he had done for her? Her distress awoke a nausea in her body and she kept moving her lips in silent fervent prayer.

A bell clanged upon her heart. She felt him seize her hand:

"Come!"

All the seas of the world tumbled about her heart. He was drawing her into them: he would drown her. She gripped with both hands at the iron railing.

"Come!"

No! No! No! It was impossible. Her hands clutched the iron in frenzy. Amid the seas she sent a cry of anguish.

"Eveline! Evvy!"

He rushed beyond the barrier and called to her to follow. He was shouted at to go on, but he still called to her. She set her white face to him; passive, like a helpless animal. Her eyes gave him no sign of love or farewell or recognition.

(252 words)

Source: Joyce, James: "Eveline". In: Joyce, James: Dubliners.
London: Grant Richards Ltd. 1914

Annotations

North Wall (l. 1): Dublin Port, located east of the city centre; nausea (l. 9): feeling of sickness; fervent (l. 10): hot, passionate; (to) clang (l. 11): (to) make a loud sound; frenzy (l. 16): state of great anxiety or excitement; anguish (l. 17): mental or physical suffering caused by extreme pain or worry

14 Read the text Part 1 and give the lines of the passage that contain the following information:

a) Although looking after the household and her younger brothers was hard work, Eveline quite liked it.
b) Eveline met her boyfriend by coincidence.
c) Going to the opera with Frank was an exciting experience for her.
d) Eveline became fond of Frank gradually; it wasn't love at first sight.
e) Eveline's father cared for his daughter when she was ill in bed.
f) Above all, Eveline wants Frank to free her from her present life.

Statement	a	b	c	d	e	f
Lines						

15 Read Part 1 again carefully and collect all information on Eveline's lover Frank. Then fill in the grid.

appearance	
character	
hobbies	

16 Now read both parts of the text and match the external action with Eveline's thoughts and feelings.

1 Eveline is sitting by the window at sunset.	A Eveline's doubts increase; she is confused and unsure if going away with Frank is still a good idea.
2 She is getting ready for the embarkation.	B Eveline believes that Frank could make her happy but at the same time she is jumpy and nervous.
3 She is amongst the crowd at the port.	C She suddenly feels caught and has the impression of being drowned by Frank.
4 Frank calls her name and takes her hand.	D With mixed feelings, she thinks about her responsibilities in the house, family life in former times and the promise she gave to her mother.
5 Eveline holds onto the railing and refuses to let go.	E Paralysed and without any emotion she watches Frank, who calls out for her again and again.

1	2	3	4	5

17 Go through the whole text again and collect the reasons Eveline has given herself for either leaving Ireland for good or staying with her family.

Reasons to leave with Frank 	• • • • •
Reasons to stay 	• • • • •

18 Decide which of these statements on Eveline's change of mind are true or false. Find the lines in the text which support your decision and give evidence.

	true	false
a) Eveline is given special treats by Frank and enjoys his attention and kindness very much.	☐	☐
Evidence: ______________________________		
b) Eveline had promised her sick mother to take care of the younger children as long as they needed her, which is why she feels guilty about leaving.	☐	☐
Evidence: ______________________________		
c) Eveline had never been at sea before, which is why she worries herself sick.	☐	☐
Evidence: ______________________________		
d) Eveline's feelings for Frank change when she identifies him as the cause of all her suffering.	☐	☐
Evidence: ______________________________		
e) In her distressed state, Frank becomes a stranger to Eveline again.	☐	☐
Evidence: ______________________________		

Father to son

by Elizabeth Jennings (1926–2001)

I do not understand this child
Though we have lived together now
In the same house for years. I know
Nothing of him, so try to build
Up a relationship from how
He was when small. Yet have I killed

The seed I spent or sown it where
The land is his and none of mine?
We speak like strangers, there's no sign
Of understanding in the air.
This child is built to my design
Yet what he loves I cannot share.

Silence surrounds us. I would have
Him prodigal, returning to
His father's house, the home he knew,
Rather than see him make and move
His world. I would forgive him too,
Shaping from sorrow a new love.

Father and son, we both must live
On the same globe and the same land.
He speaks: I cannot understand
Myself, why anger grows from grief.
We each put out an empty hand,
Longing for something to forgive.

(157 words)

Source: Recoveries *by Elizabeth Jennings, published by Andre Deutsch Ltd, London, 1964*

Annotation

prodigal (l. 14): too willing to spend money or waste time, *here:* allusion to the parable of the prodigal son (= *Gleichnis vom verlorenen Sohn, der seinen Erbteil ausgezahlt bekommt und verprasst, aber mit allen Ehren von seinem Vater empfangen wird, als er reumütig zurückkehrt)*

19 a) Choose the image that portrays the relationship between father and son best in the past respectively in the present.

b) Collect information on what is revealed about the …

… father	
… son	

20 Choose suitable adjectives to describe the mood the speaker is in. Mark them with a cross (✗).

- ☐ angry
- ☐ afraid
- ☐ desperate
- ☐ happy
- ☐ hopeless
- ☐ gloomy
- ☐ indifferent
- ☐ mad
- ☐ relieved
- ☐ sad

21 Rephrase the following passages in your own words:

a) “Yet have I killed [t]he seed I spent or sown it where [t]he land is his and none of mine?” (ll. 6–8)

____

____

____

b) “I would have [h]im prodigal […] [r]ather than see him make and move [h]is world.” (ll. 13–17)

____

____

____

c) “I would forgive him too, [s]haping from sorrow a new love.” (ll. 17/18)

____

____

____

d) “We each put out an empty hand, [l]onging for something to forgive.” (ll. 23/24)

____

____

____

Basics

Formale Gedichtanalyse

Gedichte sind nicht immer leicht zu entschlüsseln, weil ihre Aussage verkürzt ist und sie sich oft einer bildhaften Sprache bedienen. Mit den richtigen Methoden und Techniken ist die Gedichtinterpretation aber kein Hexenwerk. Solange sich die Interpretation am Text belegen lässt, gibt es kein richtig oder falsch, sondern mehrere interessante Wege.

Wie gehen Sie vor?

- Lesen Sie das Gedicht sorgfältig und mehrmals – auch lautes Lesen hilft („Klangwirkung"). Arbeiten Sie Textmarker in verschiedenen Farben. Markieren Sie Wichtiges, Unbekanntes und Unverständliches.
- Entwickeln Sie für sich eine (vorläufige) Arbeitshypothese zur Intention des Verfassers / der Verfasserin („Was will der Dichter / die Dichterin sagen?"). Das ist noch keine endgültige und abschließende Interpretation!
- **Inhaltsangabe:** Geben Sie den Inhalt mit eigenen Worten wieder, nennen Sie dabei in einem ersten „Kern-" oder „Basissatz" Verfasser*in, Thema, Sprecher*in („lyrisches Ich"), zentrale Aussage und die Verbindung zwischen Gedicht und Titel.
- **Formanalyse:** Bestimmen Sie die Form des Gedichts, die Anzahl der Strophen und Verse, das Metrum, das Reimschema und erschließen Sie die Bildsprache des Gedichts (z. B. Metaphern, Vergleiche und Symbole).
- **Interpretation:** Verdeutlichen Sie den Zusammenhang zwischen Inhalt (Aussage) und Form (z. B. die Form spiegelt die zentrale Textaussage wieder bzw. steht im Gegensatz zur Botschaft des Gedichts). Beide Elemente machen das Gedicht als lyrisches Kunstwerk aus.

22 Fill in the gaps with words from the list.

theme • image • fault • speaker • personality • contact • rhyme scheme • conflict • stanzas • form • mood • forgive • enjambments • monologue • estrangement

The ________________ of Elizabeth Jennings' poem, "Father to Son", is the generation gap. The ________________ in the poem is a disappointed and frustrated father who mourns the loss of ________________ to his son. He admits that, despite having lived under the same roof for years, he does not really know anything about the interests, dreams and aspirations of his son now. To overcome the ________________, he would like to rebuild a relationship with his son as it used to be when the boy was still young. In his ________________, the father asks himself whether he is responsible for the drifting apart. However, they do not communicate, and in a nostalgic

________________ the father wants his son to return home and be the friendly little boy again that he once was. He believes his son has done something wrong, because he says that he is ready to ________________ him and start all over again.

The poem is composed of four ________________ with six lines each, with the ________________ being a – b – b – a – b – a. The regular ________________ suggests balance and harmony, but in reality the flow of speech is constantly interrupted by numerous ________________. In this way the discrepancy between form and content mirrors the ________________ of the two generations who live in different worlds. The father uses the ________________ of the seed, which perhaps represents the love and affection which he has invested in his son. However, he is unable to understand that he cannot much influence the growth of the plant. He does not realise that times have changed and that his son has developed his own ____________.

All in all, Elizabeth Jennings makes the reader feel sorry for the father who is so deeply affected by the loss of communication with his son but, at the same time, she shows that it is not always the children's ________________ when parents and the younger generation distance themselves from each other.

Listening

Gun possession

Track 1

Read the tasks below, then listen to what Jahlil Jackson has to say.

23 Choose the statements that fit the contents of the commentary on Youthradio and mark them with a cross (✗).
Be careful, **more than one** answer might be correct.

a) When Jahlil Jackson was 12, he ...

- ☐ saw how a man was shot at the bus stop.
- ☐ held a gun in his hands for the first time.
- ☐ first thought about buying a gun.
- ☐ was threatened by a gunman.

b) Jahlil Jackson saw a man running towards him, so he ...

- ☐ hid inside the corner store.
- ☐ attempted to stop him.
- ☐ tried to get away as quickly as possible.
- ☐ called the police.

c) In the past, Jahlil Jackson ...

- ☐ could easily have bought a gun.
- ☐ did not know the right people to buy a gun.
- ☐ did not have enough money to purchase a gun.
- ☐ thought it essential to possess a gun.

d) Jahlil Jackson had his doubts about buying a gun as he was scared ...

- ☐ of a change of character.
- ☐ of having to actually use it.
- ☐ that he might end up being a murderer.
- ☐ of coming into contact with the wrong kind of people.

e) Jahlil Jackson was happy that ...
- ☐ his family moved to another state.
- ☐ his grandparents moved to a less dangerous neighbourhood.
- ☐ his family moved to another city.
- ☐ he could leave his former neighbourhood for college.

f) In his new surroundings, Jahlil ...
- ☐ feels completely safe.
- ☐ can focus on more everyday issues.
- ☐ does not need a gun anymore.
- ☐ experiences less hardship and violence.

24 Listen again, then complete the following tasks.

a) Explain what life in Jahlil Jackson's old neighbourhood was like.

b) Outline Jahlil Jackson's older cousins' attitude to guns.

c) Sum up what Jahlil Jackson's friends thought of him.

d) Explain what message Jahlil Jackson wants to convey to other young people.

British politicians on immigration

Theresa May on immigration

Annotations

Track 2

Theresa May: British Conservative politician, Home Secretary 2010–2016
cohesive: closely united
(to) plug: (to) fill

25 Listen carefully and decide whether the statements are true or false.

	true	false
a) Millions of people from poorer countries have come to live in Britain.	☐	☐
b) Theresa May wants to reduce the number of newcomers through stricter entry requirements.	☐	☐
c) The rapidly increasing numbers of immigrants challenge the stability of British society.	☐	☐
d) The most urgent measures in the years to come will be to provide housing and jobs for the immigrants.	☐	☐
e) The country is already confronted with a high unemployment rate.	☐	☐
f) The priority is for Britain to accept academic immigrants whose skills are in demand.	☐	☐
g) May's tough stand on immigration is based on findings of the OECD and the House of Commons.	☐	☐

26 Listen to the speech again and correct the mistakes in the following summary.

Summary	Errors
Theresa May predicts that 310,000 new housing facilities will have to be built next year to meet the increasing demand. In addition, 90,000 places more will be needed in schools by the year 2020.	______ ______ ______ ______

David Cameron on immigration

Annotations

Track 3

David Cameron: British Prime Minister 2010–2016
bogus: pretending to be real; a college which is only set up to enable people from overseas to apply for a British student visa
dole: money paid by the state to unemployed people
NHS: National Health Service (the public health service in Britain that provides medical treatment and is paid for by taxes)
(to) clamp down: (to) stop an illegal activity
sham: not genuine, but intended to seem real

27 Listen to David Cameron speaking and complete the missing words.

If you have uncontrolled immigration, you have uncontrolled __________ on public services. And that raises basic issues of fairness. Uncontrolled immigration can __________ our labour market and push down wages. And working people rightly want a government that is on their __________. Uncontrolled immigration means too many people coming to the UK __________ but staying illegally. And people are fed up with a system that allows those who are not __________ to be in our country to remain here. So the British people want these things __________. And as the Home Secretary's just said, we've been working over the last five years towards that. We've fundamentally taken the __________ that we inherited and changed it.

28 Mark the areas with a cross (✗) in which special background checks have taken place according to Cameron.

29 Listen to the speech again and match the beginning of each sentence (A–E) to the correct ending (1–5).

A Illegal immigrants are a burden on the state because they …	**1** are prepared to work for less money than members of the host society.
B Illegal workers are so competitive on the labour market because they …	**2** believe that social benefits should be distributed more carefully.
C The government was forced to take action as British people …	**3** come from countries outside the European Union.
D Illegal immigrants have to pay for medical treatment if they …	**4** really leave the UK when told to do so.
E There are special exit checks to make sure that immigrants …	**5** don't pay taxes as they are not registered in the system.

A	B	C	D	E

Food policy report

Track 4

This is a radio report about food policy. Read the tasks below, then listen to the report.

Annotations

The International Food Policy Research Institute: the IFPRI was founded in 1975. Its aim is to improve agricultural and food policies and promote the usage of modern agricultural technology.

family farming: farming by individuals, not by large corporations

30 Mark the correct alternative(s) with a cross (✗).

a) Shenggen Fan states that many children …

- ☐ have become refugees.
- ☐ do not have enough to eat.
- ☐ do not receive proper medical care.
- ☐ are exploited on their parents' farms.

b) The Global Food Policy Report reveals there is a connection between …

- ☐ progress and a decrease in malnutrition.
- ☐ trouble spots and an increase in hunger.
- ☐ food security and a decrease in population.
- ☐ food security and a decrease in malnutrition.

c) To illustrate climate change the director mentions:

- ☐ floods.
- ☐ hurricanes.
- ☐ heat waves.
- ☐ droughts.

d) Diseases such as Ebola influence the global food system as they bring about a …

- ☐ decrease in production.
- ☐ change of trade routes.
- ☐ different attitude to how food is selected.
- ☐ confusion of the market.

e) "Middle income countries" play a crucial role in the global food system because there, people ...

- [ ] eat food that lacks important ingredients.
- [ ] eat in an unbalanced way.
- [ ] develop eating disorders.
- [ ] still do not have enough to eat.

31 Listen to the report again and complete these sentences with a maximum of four words.

a) When it comes to children's diet, hygiene ...

____

b) The more conflicts there are in a country, the more people ...

____

c) Due to climate change the production of food ...

____

d) Refugees in African countries were particularly affected by ...

____

32 Decide which of the following statements are correct and make a cross (**✗**):

- [ ] During the Ebola crisis, many countries were reluctant to take in grain from abroad.
- [ ] In middle income countries, there are still billions of people suffering from malnutrition.
- [ ] Weight problems and deficient diets will become an even bigger problem in these countries in the future.
- [ ] Middle income countries also need to take efforts to better the situation of people living and working in rural areas.

From a teenager's perspective

Nanette Thompson talks about being an only child

Track 5

Annotations

bratty: badly behaved (brat = *Balg, Göre, Schlingel*)
sibling: brother or sister
hand-me-downs: clothes worn by older brothers or sisters
sorority: a society for female students at a university or college

33 Read the statements below, then listen to Nanette talking about her childhood on Youthradio. Decide whether the statements are true, false, or the information is not given in the text and mark the correct solution with a cross (✗).

	true	false	not given
a) Nanette's friends envied her that she did not have any brothers and sisters.	☐	☐	☐
b) She herself was quite happy to grow up as an only child.	☐	☐	☐
c) Nanette's parents decided to have only one child for financial reasons.	☐	☐	☐
d) She is looking forward to having "sisters" at college.	☐	☐	☐
e) Nanette hopes that there will be no trouble between the girls in the sorority.	☐	☐	☐

34 Listen again and complete the table with the relevant information mentioned by Nanette.

advantages of being an only child	advantages of having brothers and sisters
•	•
•	•
•	•

Teaching tech to mom by Nanette Thompson

Track 6

Annotations

(to) reverse: (to) move or turn in the opposite direction
font: *Schriftart*

35 First of all, read the tasks below, then listen to the recording on Youthradio. Mark the correct statements with a cross (✗).

a) Nanette Thompson taught her mother how to …
- ☐ use her smartphone.
- ☐ work with Powerpoint.
- ☐ use the computer.

b) She thinks that her mother is …
- ☐ making progress fast.
- ☐ still slow on the computer.
- ☐ an almost hopeless case.

c) Nanette claims that teaching technology to her mother …
- ☐ has been a disillusioning experience.
- ☐ has given her a deeper insight into the learning process itself.
- ☐ will not be an issue anymore as soon as she is off to college.

36 Listen to the recording again and complete these sentences.

a) As a digital native, Nanette knew how to work with computer ______________ although she was only ______ years old.

b) She helped her mum with a job ______________.

c) Her mother told her which fonts and colours to use by ______________ to them.

d) Nanette's mother still struggles with ______________ documents to emails or ______________ emojis to text messages.

e) Through her teaching Nanette learned how to be more ______________.

The age of smartphones

Teenagers and smartphone addiction

Track 7

Annotations

digital cleanse: taking a break from smartphones, tablets, television, video games etc.
Ziploc bag: reusable plastic bag with a zip fastener

37 Listen to the text and do the following tasks in the given order:

a) These are the names of the people you will hear about in the report:

Destiny Davis • Jarred Amato • Tony Gonzalez • Jamya Whitmore

Listen to the report for the first time and add the people's names to the right column. Then go on to task 37 b.

reporter	student	teacher

b) Mark the correct statements with a cross (✗).
Be careful, **more than one** answer might be right.

The report is about an experiment which requires students to …

- ☐ do without screen time for a week.
- ☐ give up their smartphones for a day.
- ☐ take part in a digital cleanse for a weekend.

The students are …

- ☐ totally against the experience.
- ☐ excited about the experience.
- ☐ unsure and nervous.

Jarred Amato believes that students are …

- ☐ constantly occupied with their smartphones.
- ☐ desperate to get away from their phones.
- ☐ unable to fight their smartphone addiction.

It turns out that without their phones, students have …

- ☐ the urge to talk to each other much more.
- ☐ slept more hours than usual.
- ☐ spent more time with their families.

38 Listen again and correct the mistakes in the written text.

Summary	Errors
Like Destiny Davis, some students felt good when they were not receiving any messages. For half of them, unplugging was easier then expected. Several spent time inside the family home, which had not happened for a month at least. It might be a consolation to some that the missed calls are still there on the phones to be received.	______ ______ ______ ______ ______ ______ ______

The fear of being out of phone contact

Track 8

Annotations

temptation: the desire to do sth
(to) take a toll: (to) have a negative effect
(to) hover: *here:* (to) be near at hand
resource: *here:* energy
seductive: attractive, tempting
(to) be calibrated to entice: (to) be meant to provoke sb to do sth
MIT: Massachusetts Institute of Technology, famous for scientific and technical research
gratification: satisfaction
(to) accomplish: (to) do or complete sth
punter: a person who gambles
rush: a sudden thrill
substitution: the act of replacing one thing or person with another

39 Listen to the report and decide which of the two paragraphs summarises it best.

A The comment is about the damage technology addiction might have on your physical and mental health. People are constantly under the impression that their phone is ringing or receiving text messages. They even have trouble sleeping next to their phone. As a consequence, they are unable to concentrate on work.

B The comment is about how to resist the temptation of looking at your smartphone. The human brain is unable to do too many things at the same time. Trying not to check your phone requires so much energy that you are unable to perform difficult tasks properly. As a result, the commentator advises you to switch your phone off from time to time.

40 Listen to the recording again and match the sentence halves that go together.

1 More than 50 % of British people …	A switch rapidly between tasks.
2 Their brain subconsciously wants to …	B avoid the more difficult ones.
3 People who resisted temptations before …	C check their smartphone constantly.
4 To satisfy their needs, modern users …	D are more likely to give up on difficult tasks later on.
5 Doing many things at the same time …	E suffer from nomophobia.
6 By focusing on smaller, less important issues people …	F results in doing nothing properly.

1	2	3	4	5	6

Dating habits

British people's dating habits

Track 9

41 Listen to the report and mark the correct statements with a cross (✗).

a) Relationships of people who have met online are …

- [ ] less stable than those of partners who have met offline.
- [ ] more stable than those of partners who have met offline.
- [ ] as stable as those of partners who have met offline.

b) Since 2005, people's attitude to online dating has …

- [ ] not changed at all.
- [ ] become more positive.
- [ ] become more negative.

c) Match.com is a leading online dating service which …

- [ ] is represented in over 50 countries.
- [ ] is used by over 70 million people.
- [ ] was launched at the beginning of the 21st century.

d) Most people who use online dating services work in …

- [ ] jobs that require a lot of travelling.
- [ ] the industrial sector.
- [ ] jobs that require a high level of education.

e) A successful profile contains words like …

- [ ] dog, soda, comedy.
- [ ] explore, chat, yoga.
- [ ] yoga, comedy, dog.

42 Listen to the report again and fill in the missing words and numbers.

It is estimated that one in five new relationships and one in ____________ marriages now begins online. A recent study found that marriages that start online are ____________ more likely to ____________ than those between couples who met through more traditional means. And while a ____________ of people surveyed in ____________ described online dating as "desperate", that figure has ____________ to less than a ________ today. Since dating juggernaut match.com launched back in ___________ more than ___________ million people have logged onto the service which is accessible in ___________ countries.

Source: Sarah Rainey, Lauren Alpe; on: www.telegraph.co.uk, 11th February 2015

American teens' dating habits

Track 10

Annotations

(to) get up to speed: (to) get up to date
padlock: a portable lock for fastening doors or boxes etc.
(to) gravitate: (to) move towards, (to) be attracted to
(to) prune: (to) clean up, remove
(to) ensue: (to) follow

43 Listen to the report and match the sentence halves that go together.

A	Half of teenagers aged 13 to 17 have used social media to …	1	let others know that someone is currently not in a relationship.
B	The online biography is used to …	2	said social media makes them feel closer to their partner.
C	Less than 10 per cent of the teenagers interviewed …	3	prefer saying it personally to using electronic devices.
D	Unlike most of the girls, sixty-five per cent of the boys …	4	let somebody else know they have a crush on them.
E	When it comes to breaking up with a partner, most teenagers …	5	claim to have met their partner online.

A	B	C	D	E

44 Read the statements below, then listen to the report again. Decide whether the statements are true, false, or the information is not given in the report.

	true	false	not given
a) Social media play an important role in starting romances.	☐	☐	☐
b) Chinatown Metro stop in Washington is a popular place for teenagers to meet after school.	☐	☐	☐
c) The emojis used indicate how serious a relationship is.	☐	☐	☐
d) Though few teenagers have met their current partner online, social media is used for flirting a lot.	☐	☐	☐
e) Facebook is the preferred site for teenagers to flirt or maintain relationships.	☐	☐	☐
f) The number of adults having an account with Snapchat or Instagram is rising.	☐	☐	☐
g) An increasing number of teenagers pick their partner to gain admiration from their peers.	☐	☐	☐
h) Parents should worry less about what their teens are doing on social media.	☐	☐	☐

Mediation

German – Englisch

Mit beiden Beinen im Salat

Die besten Kräuter wachsen zwischen Parkbuchten und im Kreisverkehr: Auf Tour mit Zürichs dienstältestem Guerillagärtner.

Von Jessica Braun

Wenn Maurice Maggi frische Zutaten zum Kochen braucht, geht er auf den Friedhof Zürich-Sihlfeld. Der ist zugleich der größte Park der Stadt, nur ein Drittel der Fläche wird als Begräbnisstätte genutzt. Die Verwaltung baute Ende der fünfziger Jahre die „Betreten verboten"-Schilder vor den Wiesen ab, seither darf man zwischen turmhohen Tannen picknicken und dösen. Oder, wie Maurice Maggi, Wildpflanzen für das Mittagessen sammeln. An diesem Morgen sind alle Zutaten frisch gewaschen, Tau haftet an jedem Grashalm. Maggi holt einen Beutel hervor. Darin sind Lindenblätter und -blüten, wir haben sie auf dem Weg hierher gepflückt. Jetzt streckt Maggi sich nach jungen Tannennadelspitzen, behutsam zupft er die hellen Quasten vorne an den Zweigen ab. Sie sollen dem Risotto Struktur geben.

Maurice Maggi ist gelernter Gärtner, kochte aber immer schon gern. Später vertauschte er Beruf und Hobby, stand als Chef hinter dem Herd und ging seinem früheren Beruf vor allem heimlich nach: Seit 1984 flaniert er mit einem Säckchen Blumensamen in der Tasche durch die Straßen. Der 58-Jährige ist Guerillagärtner, ein Urgestein der Bewegung. In 30 Jahren hat er Zürichs Stadtbild verwildert, nun nutzt er den Wildwuchs, um die heimische Küche zu revolutionieren. Mit Zutaten, die exotisch schmecken, aber vor der Haustür wachsen: Giersch und Ackersenf, Schlüsselblumen und Malvensamen, Eibenbeeren und Berberitzen. [...] Saisonal aufgebaut und regional verwurzelt, macht es sich gut im biobourgeoisen Küchenregal. Für Maggi zählt jedoch, dass die (Un-)Kräuter, die er zum Kochen verwendet, für jedermann verfügbar sind. „Sie kosten nichts. In wirtschaftlich schwierigen Zeiten sollte man das nicht außer Acht lassen."

Zürich durch seine Augen zu sehen bedeutet meist, den Blick zu senken. Vor Fotomotiven bleibt er nicht stehen, ihn fasziniert das Lebendige. Die Eselsdistel in der Zypressenstrasse etwa, die vom Friedhof in Richtung Norden führt. Hier haben Stadtgärtner neue Bäume zwischen die Parkbuchten gesetzt. Noch wirken sie mickrig, auch wegen der Pflanzen, die neben ihnen sprießen.

Maggi hat die „Baumscheiben“, so nennen Guerillagärtner das normalerweise erdbraune Rund um den Stamm, mit seinen Samenmischungen okkupiert. Einige metallisch gefärbte Stängel überragen bereits die umstehenden Autos. Voll Vaterstolz beugt er sich über eine Knospe. „Eselsdisteln gehören in der Schweiz zu den gefährdeten Arten.“ Der Sauerampfer ist sogar über mich hinausgewachsen: Ich könnte die Blätter im Stehen abkauen. Und dürfte das auch, gemäß der Regeln, die mir Maggi mitgegeben hat: Blätter und Blüten vom Wegesrand solle ich nur nehmen, wenn sie höher wachsen, als ein Hund sein Bein heben kann. Pflanzen, die weiter als fünf Meter von Wegen entfernt wachsen, „kann man in Zürich immer unbedenklich ernten“. In den Parks gilt Leinenpflicht – länger als fünf Meter seien die selten.

[...] Sauerampfer findet in der Gourmetküche zunehmend Verwendung, in Zürich, einer der teuersten Metropolen der Welt, kann ein Wildkräutersalat im Restaurant schon mal 30 Euro kosten.

[...] Wir folgen der Sihlfeldstrasse von Kräuterinsel zu Kräuterinsel. Maggi zeigt mir blau blühenden Borretsch, Zichorien, die an Kornblumen erinnern, die verschachtelten Hüte von Akelei und die Blüten-Tutus des Spitzwegerichs. Wir naschen vom Ackersenf, dessen Blüten den Biss junger Erbsen haben und nach Milch und Wasabi schmecken. Vor dem Café Du Bonheur am Bullingerplatz bleibt Maggi stehen. „Hier verlief die Stadtautobahn“, erklärt er, jetzt gilt Tempo 20. Um den Verkehr noch stärker zu beruhigen, haben Anwohner Teile des Kreisverkehrs mit Blumenkübeln zugestellt, die Stadtverwaltung lässt sie bisher gewähren. Dieser Akt zivilen Ungehorsams hat aus der Straße eine bunte Gartenterrasse gemacht, Maggi hat hier gemeinsam mit Schülern essbare Pflanzen gesät.

Als Junge hätte er manchmal gern mehr zu essen gehabt. Mit acht Jahren verlor er seinen Vater durch einen Unfall, die Mutter zog mit den sieben Kindern in einen Vorort von Zürich. Das Geld war knapp, Wildpflanzen zu sammeln war selbstverständlich. [...] *(604 Wörter)*

Quelle: Jessica Braun, in: Die ZEIT, *Ausgabe 25/2014*

Basics

Sprachmittlung

Wenn Sie gebeten werden, eine Sprachmittlung anzufertigen, liegen Ihnen in der Regel ein bis zwei Texte in der Ausgangssprache vor (u. U. auch ein Text und ein visueller Impuls in Form einer Statistik, eines Bildes oder eines Werbeplakats). Die in diesen Texten und Materialien enthaltenen Informationen sollen dann **von einer in die andere Sprache übertragen** werden. Meist werden Sie aufgefordert, deutsche Informationen ins Englische zu „mitteln“.

Wie gehen Sie vor?

- Stellen Sie zunächst sicher, dass Sie das Original gut verstanden haben.
- In der Regel wird Ihnen in der Aufgabenstellung bereits eine **konkrete Situation** vorgegeben, die es erfordert, dass Bestandteile des (deutschen) Textes ins Englische übertragen werden, z. B. weil Sie Inhalte eines deutschen Zeitungsartikels an Ihren amerikanischen Brieffreund weitergeben möchten (siehe Aufgabe 45).
- Die **Länge des Zieltextes** wird Ihnen in der Aufgabenstellung vorgegeben, meist sind es ca. 250 Wörter. In jedem Fall müssen Sie den Ausgangstext zusammenfassen. Anhand des Kontextes, in den die Sprachmittlungsaufgabe eingebettet ist, sollten Sie deshalb zwischen wichtigen und unwichtigen Passagen des Ausgangsmaterials unterscheiden: Lassen Sie also Details und Randinformationen beiseite und konzentrieren Sie sich auf das Wesentliche. Oft sind Ihnen in der Aufgabenstellung schon wichtige Aspekte vorgegeben, die Sie berücksichtigen sollten, z. B. werden Sie in Aufgabe 45 gebeten, darauf einzugehen, was die Guerillagärtner in Europa bereits erreicht haben.
- Neben dem Kontext wird Ihnen auch die **Textsorte** vorgegeben. Bei dem Text, den Sie in Aufgabe 45 verfassen sollen, handelt es sich z. B. um eine Zusammenfassung. Daher müssen Sie wesentliche Merkmale dieser Textsorte berücksichtigen, wenn Sie Ihren Zieltext verfassen (Verwendung des *present tense*, Verwenden der 3. Person Singular, keine direkte Rede etc.). **Informationen zu speziellen Textsorten** finden Sie im Kapitel „Writing“.
- Ausgehend von dem Zielpublikum, für das Sie der Aufgabenstellung nach Ihre Sprachmittlung verfassen, können **Sprache und Stil** Ihres Textes stark zwischen Umgangssprache (z. B. in der E-Mail an eine Freundin) und gehobener Sprache (z. B. im Leserbrief) variieren.
- Denken Sie daran, in Ihrem Text generell **eigene Formulierungen** zu verwenden. Es genügt nicht, wichtige Passagen aus dem Ausgangstext zu übersetzen. Verwenden Sie Synonyme oder Umschreibungen, um einen authentischen Text zu erstellen.

45 Your American e-pal is a member of Green Guerillas, a community gardening organisation in New York City. By chance, you have spotted the article printed above in your parents' weekly newspaper. As you believe your friend might be interested to hear about the achievements of European guerilla gardeners, you sum up the article for him.

a) Before you start writing, collect information on the following items:
   - the person portrayed in the article,
   - his occupations (i. e. his profession and what he does in his free time),
   - his intentions,
   - how his guerilla activities are received by Zurich society.

b) Put the ideas into a suitable order first, then write a summary of about 200 words.

Ich hab's gemacht

Der Junge, der Afrika erleuchten will

Mit 14 Jahren baute er aus Schrott ein Windrad. So wurde ein Junge aus Malawi zum Helden für Wissenschaftler und Entwicklungspolitiker. Weil er nicht auf Wunder wartete.

[...] Er ist groß, schlaksig, lächelt schüchtern. Vor ihm im Dunkeln sitzt das Publikum der „TED-Konferenz“. Das Kürzel steht für „Technology, Entertainment, Design“, es ist ein elitärer Zirkel von Wissenschaftlern, Künstlern, Erfindern aus aller Welt, jedes Jahr treffen sie sich, um Visionäre wie Al Gore oder Stephen Hawking über ihre Ideen sprechen zu hören.

Und jetzt steht da dieser Junge. William Kamkwamba, 19, aus Malawi, Sohn eines Tabakbauern. Mit 14 ist er von der Schule geflogen, weil die Eltern das Schulgeld nicht mehr zahlen konnten, eine Hungersnot hatte die Ersparnisse aufgezehrt. Doch dann hatte der Junge diesen verrückten Plan, der das Leben in seinem Dorf von Grund auf änderte. Ein Blogger schrieb darüber, so landete er hier.

„William, deine Idee vor fünf Jahren“, sagt der Moderator und lächelt, „worum ging's da?“ „Ich wollte ein Windrad bauen.“ „Um Strom zu gewinnen für Licht und Wasser?“ „Yeah.“ „Wie hast du das gemacht?“ Der Junge schwitzt, er spricht nur gebrochen Englisch, doch er pflügt sich durch die Sätze: „Ich ... ging in die Bücherei ... sehe mir ein Buch übers Windradmachen an ... ich versuch's ...“ – breites Grinsen – „ ... hab's gemacht!“ Das Publikum tobt.

Seit diesem Satz ist William Kamkwamba ein Held – nicht nur in Malawi, diesem schmalen Landstreifen im Südosten Afrikas, sondern unter Wissenschaftlern und Entwicklungspolitikern auf der ganzen Welt: Ein Teenie, der nicht auf Wunder wartet, sondern kurzerhand selbst die Dinge regelt – ist es nicht das, was Afrika, ach was, die ganze Welt, braucht? Das Video von Williams Auftritt wird im Internet tausendfach aufgerufen. Er wird zum „World Economic Forum“ eingeladen. Das *Wallstreet Journal* widmet ihm eine Titelstory. [...]

Als er [...] die Schule verlassen muss, entdeckt William die Dorfbücherei. Zum Lesen der zerfledderten Lehrbücher reicht sein Englisch kaum, doch mit Hilfe der Bilder erschließt er sich das Funktionieren von Magneten und Motoren. Und er begreift: Die „großen, weißen Türme mit drei Flügeln“ auf dem Einband seines Lieblingsbuchs sind eigentlich Windräder! Man kann mit ihnen Strom erzeugen, also auch Radios, Glühbirnen oder Wasserpumpen betreiben.

Monatelang plündert er den Schrottplatz des Dorfes, schwatzt seinem Vater das Familienfahrrad ab und bastelt schließlich unter den misstrauischen Blicken der Nachbarn („Der kleine Kamkwamba kifft zu viel!“) aus Abflussrohren, Fahrradteilen und einem Traktorgebläse ein Windrad. Gefährlich schwankt das Gerüst im Steppenwind, fast fackelt William mit dem Strom die Hütte seiner Eltern ab. Doch zum ersten Mal haben die Kamkwambas nun elektrisches Licht. Die Nachbarn stehen Schlange, um ihre Handys aufzuladen. [...]

Wer den Windradjungen heute treffen will, muss sich durch den Stau von Johannesburg kämpfen. In Honeydew, einem der besseren Vororte im Norden der südafrikanischen Metropole, liegt der Campus der „African Leadership Academy“. Die Schule ist eine private Bildungsoase, gesäumt von Birken und Trauerweiden, zwischen Backsteingebäuden stolzieren Pfaue. Hier holt William Kamkwamba [...] das Abitur nach. Die 20 000 Dollar, die das kostet, zahlt die Schule. Das ist ihr Prinzip. Gesponsert unter anderem von Boston Consulting sollen hier Ausnahmetalente aus ganz Afrika unter Idealbedingungen die Hochschulreife erlangen. Dafür wird erwartet, dass sie nach dem Studium für mindestens zehn Jahre in Afrika arbeiten, den Kontinent durch neue Ideen voranbringen. Sonst muss das Stipendium zurückgezahlt werden. *(520 Wörter)*

Quelle: Kristina Maroldt, in: Frankfurter Allgemeine Sonntagszeitung

46 You are currently doing an internship at the German branch of Boston Consulting, the company that paid for William Kamkwamba's education. In the meantime, William has successfully graduated from Dartmouth College in Hanover, New Hampshire.
Boston Consulting is very proud of his achievements and asked you to write an article about his success story for their international website, which presents several investment projects in the Third World.

a) In preparation for this task, you have found the newspaper article printed above on the Internet. Divide the text up into sections and provide each section with a suitable heading.

b) Then write an article of about 300 words that illustrates William Kamkwamba's success story. Provide your text with a suitable heading and do not forget to present the involvement of Boston Consulting in a favourable light.

Überleben üben in den Everglades

Im Everglades-Nationalpark kann man sich mit einem Trainer auf das Ende der Welt vorbereiten. Und muss sich mit echten Plagen herumschlagen.

Von Josefine Köhn

Man kann sich Angenehmeres vorstellen, als in der Mittagshitze Treibholz zu einem Feuerplatz zu schleppen. Aber Charley Hogwood kennt keine Gnade. „Ohne Feuer kein Essen, kein Schutz, kein Wasser. Wir proben schließlich für den Ernstfall", sagt Hogwood. Bevor getrunken werden darf, muss also erst das Wasser abgekocht werden; alternativ kann man es durch ein Baumwolltuch filtern. Zeit braucht beides. Aber die Zeit hat hier, in den Everglades, ihr eigenes Maß. „Der Sumpf ist ein großartiges Gebiet, um in die Vergangenheit zu reisen. Es gibt kaum einen Ort, an dem man sich weiter von der Zivilisation entfernen kann", hatte Hogwood schon zur Begrüßung gesagt, er, der Mann, der als Überlebenstrainer in den Sümpfen arbeitet.

Tatsächlich hat es in dem 6 000 Quadratkilometer großen Nationalpark vor Millionen Jahren kaum anders ausgesehen als heute: Am Horizont scheint das wogende Sägegras in den Himmel zu wachsen. Durchbrochen wird die Wasserfläche von tief wurzelnden Mangroven, die zu kleinen Inseln zusammenwachsen, den Hammocks. Hier und da gibt es einen Sandstrand, an dem man mit dem Kajak anlegen kann. Die Wildnis hat kommerzielle Anbieter auf die Idee gebracht, Überlebenstrainings-Touren anzubieten. Vor allem bei sogenannten Preppern, Menschen, die sich auf das Ende der Zivilisation vorbereiten, gelten die Sümpfe als ideales Übungsgelände, um dem Weltuntergang gelassener entgegenzusehen.

Tewawki nennen sie die Zeit danach: The end of the world as we know it. [...] Die Vorstellung, was alles zu Tewawki führen könnte, ist schier unbegrenzt: Ein Hurrikan, eine Flut, ein Weltkrieg, der Zusammenbruch des Wirtschaftssystems, eine Pandemie, ein Atomunfall, die Polarschmelze oder gleich alles zusammen. [...] Geschätzt drei bis vier Millionen US-Amerikaner fühlen und handeln so: Sie lagern nicht nur Vorräte ein für den nächsten Hurrikan, sondern bereiten sich auf das Überleben in einer Welt ohne jegliche Infrastruktur vor.

Von ungefähr kommt diese Angst vor der Unberechenbarkeit der Natur nicht. In Miami gehören Wirbelstürme ebenso zum Jahresrhythmus wie Weihnachten oder Ostern. Sich darauf so gut es geht vorzubereiten, lernen Amerikaner schon früh.

Wie viele Prepper in den Everglades trainieren, wissen die Angestellten der Parkverwaltung nicht. „Die Prepper stellen sich bei uns nicht als solche vor“, sagt David Hooper, Parkranger und Sprecher des National Park Services. „Aber so lange sie nicht gegen die Regeln verstoßen, Bäume fällen oder die Natur zerstören, haben wir mit ihnen kein Problem.“ [...]

Mit der Natur leben, nicht gegen sie – das ist es dann auch, was die Kursteilnehmer in der Prepper-Schulung lernen sollen. Und das sieht dann, etwa beim Reiskochen, so aus: Das Feuer entfacht Hogwood mit einem metallenen Feuerstahl und ein paar Spänen [...].

Hogwood hat ein paar Bambus-Rohre zurechtgeschnitten, in denen der mitgebrachte Reis gekocht wird. Als Beilage gibt es Sägegras. Die Blattenden sind essbar, müssen aber erst mit der gebotenen Vorsicht vom Blattrand – seine Kanten sind scharf wie ein Taschenmesser – abgelöst werden. Auch die gelben Wasserlilien und einige Beeren sind essbar, allerdings „muss man schon genau wissen, was man pflückt“, sagt Hogwood. [...]

Wie lange das noch möglich sein wird, ist allerdings fraglich. Seit 1979 gehören die Everglades zum Weltnaturerbe der Unesco; sie sind jedoch als gefährdet eingestuft. Abwässer aus überdüngten Feldern gelangen in solchen Mengen in die Sümpfe, dass selbst der natürliche Filtermechanismus eines so gigantischen Gebiets nicht mehr funktioniert. Auch eingeschleppte Tier- und Pflanzenarten stören das Ökosystem. [...] Noch werden mehr als 40 Säugetier- und 350 Vogelarten in den Sümpfen gezählt, doch „verschiedene Mäusearten, Waschbären oder auch Störche sehen wir nur noch selten“, sagt Parkranger David Hooper. [...] Menschen, die sich durch die Sümpfe kämpfen, erleben indes andere Everglades-Bewohner als Plage: Es gibt hier 43 verschiedene Moskito-Arten. [...]

(587 Wörter)

Nähere Informationen

Unterkunft: Ivey House, 107 Camellia Street, Everglades City, Doppelzimmer ab 160 Euro, Tel.: 001/877/567 06 79, www.iveyhouse.com. Wer die Everglades-Tour mit Urlaub am Meer verbinden möchte: Island Bay Ressort, Zimmer ab 188 Euro, 92530 Overseas Highway, Tavernier, Key Largo, www.islandbayresort.com. Direkt am Wasser liegt der Flamingo Campground, 1 Flamingo Lodge Highway, Flamingo, Telefon: 001/239/695 01 24

Kajaktouren: Kajaks können vor Ort gemietet werden, z. B. über www.evergladesnationalparkboattoursflamingo.com; geführte Touren und Kajaks auch bei www.evergladesareatours.com; Kontakt zu Charley Hogwood: www.readygoprep.com

Weitere Auskünfte: www.visitflorida.com, Nationalpark: www.nps.gov/ever

Quelle: Josefine Köhn, in: Süddeutsche Zeitung, *19. März 2015*

47 You are planning to visit your cousin in Florida over the summer holidays, who has suggested spending some days prepping in the Everglades. As you have never heard of this activity before, you have started to do some research on the Internet and have found the article printed above.

a) First collect positive and negative aspects of experiencing a "prepper's" life.

Advantages of a prepper's life	Disadvantages of a prepper's life

b) Then write an e-mail of about 250 words, in which you refer to your cousin's suggestion and tell her what you think about it. You should also take into account the additional information for interested travellers provided by the newspaper.

Das Ende des Konsumwahns: Leben zum Nulltarif?

Text 1: Das Experiment mit dem Nichts

München ist eine teure Stadt – aber nicht für Marius Diab. Der Kunststudent ist im Konsumstreik. Er gibt seit einem Jahr kaum mehr Geld aus.

VON ELSBETH FÖGER

Marius kann nie vergessen, was auf seinem Einkaufszettel steht. Er kauft nämlich nichts ein. Keine Uni-Folder, keine Schuhe, kein Sandwich in der Mittagspause. Irgendwann hat er sich entschieden, überhaupt nichts mehr zu konsumieren.

Das geschah nicht plötzlich. Es begann damit, dass Marius keine neue Kleidung mehr nachkaufte, und endete damit, dass er im Monat nur noch Geld für eine Falafel ausgab. Als ihm auffiel, wie anspruchslos er lebte, befand Marius: Zeit für einen kompromisslosen Konsumstreik. Um ein Bewusstsein dafür zu schaffen, dass man sich problemlos mit dem versorgen kann, was andere wegwerfen.

Marius war geschockt, wie viel Essen in München im Abfall landet – etwa die Papaya, tausend Kilometer gereist, um noch völlig verzehrbar weggeworfen zu werden. Mit seiner Aktion will der Münchner gegen Ressourcenverschwendung und Konsumwahn protestieren. „Auf ein Problem aufmerksam machen funktioniert besser, wenn man etwas konsequent macht“, sagt Marius. Missionieren will er trotzdem nicht. Ein Experiment sollte es sein.

Mittlerweile lebt Marius, 25, schon seit mehr als einem Jahr so. Nur für zwei Sachen gibt der Münchner Geld aus: für seine Krankenversicherung und den Semesterbeitrag der Universität. Selbst das Dach über seinem Kopf ist kostenfrei, seit er in der Firmenwohnung eines Freundes lebt. [...]

Dass er aus dem Experiment nicht hungrig herausgeht, dafür sorgt das Freiwilligennetz „Foodsharing“. Vor zwei Jahren hat Marius das Projekt in München mitorganisiert. Das Prinzip: Betriebe oder Privatpersonen verschenken übrig gebliebene Nahrungsmittel. „Foodsaver“ nennen sich die mehr als 400 Freiwilligen, die das Essen abholen – und damit „retten“, wie sie sagen. Was mit den Nahrungsmitteln passiert, entscheidet jeder selbst. Nur verkaufen oder wegwerfen darf man sie nicht.

[...] Marius [...] verteilt die Foodsharing-Produkte zum Teil weiter, behält aber auch einiges für sich selbst. Nimmt er Bedürftigen damit nicht etwas weg? Nein, sagt er entschieden. Die Bahnhofsmission etwa hat Foodsharing-Spenden sogar abgelehnt. Und abgelaufene Sachen wollten viele Obdachlose nicht essen, das habe er bei einer Verschenk-Aktion auf der Straße bemerkt. [...]

Bei richtig großem Hunger isst Marius auch vom stehen gelassenen Gemüseauflauf. Oder von der liegen gebliebenen Currywurst. Eigentlich ist er Veganer – doch bevor etwas verschwendet wird, greift er auch bei Fleisch zu. [...] In den vielen Unannehmlichkeiten, die sich aus seinem Lebensstil ergeben, sieht Marius Vorteile. Er schränke sich gerne ein.

Kopfwehtabletten? Braucht er nicht. Zahnpasta? Bekommt er aus dem Umsonst-Laden in München, in dem man gespendete Gebrauchsgegenstände kostenlos abholen kann. Internet? Dafür nützt er das kostenfreie WLAN an der Uni. Reisen? Das klappt per Anhalter. Sein Handy kann nur Anrufe empfangen, keine tätigen. Sogar in kostenpflichtige Museen zieht es den Kunststudenten nicht. Kritisch wurde es erst vor ein paar Monaten, als Marius' Rad unerwartet kaputt ging. Er glaubte schon fast, das Experiment abbrechen zu müssen – bis er sich von einem Fahrradladen alte Bremsklötze schenken ließ.

[...] Ein kompromissloser Lebensstil, der zumindest im Kleinen auch Bekannte inspiriert: Ein Freund mit kaputtem Smartphone habe gerade darauf verzichtet, sich ein neues anzuschaffen. [...] *(469 Wörter)*

Quelle: Elsbeth Föger, in: Süddeutsche Zeitung, *20. Juli 2015*

Text 2: Supermärkte müssen unverkaufte Lebensmittel spenden

Die französische Nationalversammlung will mit einer neuen gesetzlichen Regelung die Verschwendung von Lebensmitteln reduzieren.

Die französische Nationalversammlung hat einstimmig entschieden, dass große Supermärkte künftig nicht verkaufte Lebensmittel nicht mehr wegwerfen dürfen. Die Abgeordneten haben der Verabschiedung von drei Zusatzartikeln zu einem bereits bestehenden Gesetz zugestimmt.

Einem Bericht der französischen Nachrichtenagentur AFP zufolge müssen Supermärkte nun Lebensmittel, die noch essbar sind, entweder an Wohlfahrtsorganisationen spenden, kostenlos als Tierfutter oder als Kompost für die Landwirtschaft zur Verfügung stellen.

„Es ist skandalös zu sehen, dass essbare Lebensmittel in den Müll geworfen werden", sagte Guillaume Garot, Abgeordneter der Sozialisten im französischen Parlament. Die neue Regelung betrifft alle Supermärkte, die größer als 400 Quadratmeter sind. Sie müssen nun Vereinbarungen mit karitativen Einrichtungen treffen.

Die Regierung möchte die Verschwendung von Lebensmitteln bis 2025 halbieren. Ob der Vorstoß des Parlaments in bedeutsamem Maß dazu beiträgt, ist allerdings umstritten. In Frankreich stammen nur fünf Prozent der Lebensmittelabfälle von den großen Handelsketten. Dagegen wirft jeder Franzose pro Jahr zwanzig bis dreißig Kilo Essen weg. *(151 Wörter)*

Quelle: dayk (AFP), in: Süddeutsche Zeitung, *22. Mai 2015*

48 You keep an online journal about interesting news for students. Write a blog entry in which you inform your readers about how the German student Marius Diab tries to manage living in an expensive city.

a) First put the statements below in chronological order.

Statement	Order
A The new legislation applies to all larger supermarkets.	
B Many people are afraid to eat food that is past its best-before date.	
C A lot of food is thrown away although it is perfectly edible.	
D In France, edible surplus food has to be given to charity or must be reused as animal food or in farming.	
E Organisations like Foodsaver collect food that is not wanted anymore.	
F It is the aim of the government to cut the wastage of food by half.	
G Leading a life like Marius's creates many challenges in everyday life.	
H However, with their 5 per cent share, supermarkets are responsible for only a tiny amount of the food that is thrown away every year.	
I Refusing to consume is a way of protesting against mass consumption and a senseless waste of resources.	

b) Then write a blog entry of about 250 words and make sure to put your opinion across to your readers. You should also refer to the second text about an approach taken by the French parliament to promote a more sustainable way of handling surplus food. Assess whether this strategy might be of use in Germany as well to support the poor or minimalists like Marius Diab.

Kenn dein Limit vs. Schockbilder für Raucher

Text: Schockbilder sollen Raucher abschrecken

VON CLAUS HECKING

Die Uniformschachtel für Zigaretten kommt nach Europa. Irland steht als erster EU-Staat kurz davor, das sogenannte Plain Packaging einzuführen: standardisierte, schlammbraune Verpackungen für Tabakwaren ohne Markenlogos, die fast ausschließlich aus Schockfotos und Warnhinweisen bestehen. In der Nacht zu Freitag votierte das Unterhaus in Dublin für einen entsprechenden Gesetzesentwurf der Regierung. Gesundheitsminister James O´Reilly sprach von einem historischen Schritt. Zwar muss das Oberhaus in der kommenden Woche noch zustimmen, dies gilt aber nur noch als Formsache. In zwei Jahren soll die neue Norm in Kraft treten.

Bislang schreibt Australien als einziger Staat der Welt den Zigarettenherstellern Plain Packaging vor. Eine Reihe anderer Nationen wollen nun aber nachziehen, unter anderem Frankreich, Norwegen, Neuseeland oder die Türkei. Großbritanniens Regierung will das Unterhaus noch vor den Neuwahlen im Mai über die Standardschachteln abstimmen lassen. Auf diesen immer gleich aussehenden Verpackungen darf der Markenname nur noch klein und in einer vorgegebenen Einheitsschrift gedruckt werden. Jede individuelle Farbgebung oder Werbehinweise sind verboten.

Nichts fürchten die Tabakmultis so sehr wie Plain Packaging. Hunderte Milliarden Dollar haben Konzerne wie Philip Morris International (Marlboro), Imperial Tobacco (Gauloises) oder British American Tobacco (Lucky Strike) in den Aufbau ihrer Weltmarken gesteckt. Die Schachtel ist einer der letzten Orte, auf denen sie in vielen Staaten noch mehr oder weniger frei für ihre Produkte werben können. Es geht ums ganz große Geld. Pro Jahr erwirtschaftet die internationale Tabakindustrie geschätzte 700 Milliarden Dollar Umsatz. An den Folgen des Rauchens sterben täglich geschätzte 15 000 Menschen.

Schon vor der Entscheidung des Dubliner Unterhauses hatte der Konzern JTI (Benson & Hedges) angekündigt, man werde die Regierung verklagen. Philip Morris droht der britischen Regierung mit einem Prozess vor einem internationalen Schiedsgericht. Vor einem dieser umstrittenen Gerichtshöfe hat der weltgrößte private Tabakhersteller bereits Australien auf Schadenersatz in Milliardenhöhe verklagt.

[...] Die Konzerne sehen ihre Eigentumsrechte bedroht. Zudem, so argumentieren sie, bewege die Einheitsverpackung Raucher nicht zum Aufhören, sondern fördere nur Preiskämpfe, Schmuggel und Produktpiraterie.

Tabakgegner hingegen fordern schon seit Jahren die Uniformschachtel. „Viele Zigarettenverpackungen sprechen besonders Kinder und Jugendliche an“, sagt die Heidelberger Krebsforscherin und Tabakgegnerin Martina Pötschke-Langer. „Mit Plain Packaging verliert dieses tödliche Produkt seinen Status und seine Attraktivität.“

Ob und wo die Einheitsschachtel kommt, werden am Ende wohl die Richter entscheiden – allen voran die des Europäischen Gerichtshofes (EuGH). [...]

(372 Wörter)

Quelle: Claus Hecking, in: ZEIT Online*, 27. Februar 2015*

Anmerkung der Redaktion: *Mittlerweile haben zahlreiche weitere Staaten das „plain packaging“ eingeführt. In Deutschland sind die Schockbilder nun ebenfalls üblich, wenn auch weiterhin auf Markenschachteln.*

Material: Kampagnenbild der Bundeszentrale für gesundheitliche Aufklärung (BZgA)

Mit freundlicher Genehmigung und Unterstützung der Bundeszentrale für gesundheitliche Aufklärung

49 Your English teacher asks you to collect material for a discussion on measures to prevent young people from consuming drugs such as alcohol or cigarettes. On the Internet, you have found the article printed above as well as a poster by the German "Bundeszentrale für gesundheitliche Aufklärung" (BZgA).
Use the two materials to prepare a discussion statement of about 250 words in which you decide which strategy is more effective to keep teenagers away from drugs.

a) First sum up what is understood by "plain packaging".

b) Then list advantages and disadvantages of plain packaging.

Advantages of plain packaging	Disadvantages of plain packaging

c) Describe the poster focusing on alcohol consumption amongst teenagers and analyse the message that it is intended to convey.

d) Afterwards, write a speech of about 250 words. At the end of your text, judge the efficiency of the two strategies presented.

English – German

Fighting obesity

Text: British doctors demand tax on sugary drinks

By Sarah Boseley

Britain's doctors are calling for the government to impose a 20 % tax on sugar-sweetened drinks to pay for subsidies on fruit and vegetables in an effort to slow the obesity epidemic.

A report from the British Medical Association (BMA) demands tough regulatory action on a whole range of issues, from taxation to a clampdown on the marketing of unhealthy food and drinks to children, mandatory standards on the food available in all schools and bans on clusters of fast food outlets.

"Doctors are increasingly concerned about the impact of poor diet, which is responsible for up to 70,000 deaths a year, and has the greatest impact on the NHS budget, costing £ 6 bn annually," said Prof Sheila Hollins, chair of the BMA board of science. "While sugar-sweetened drinks are very high in calories they are of limited nutritional value and when people in the UK are already consuming far too much sugar, we are increasingly concerned about how they contribute towards conditions like diabetes."

Other countries have begun to experiment with sugar taxes – the most wide-reaching of which is in Mexico. Although it is set at 10 %, public health experts have recently reported that it is having an effect. Berkeley in California also brought in a tax recently, after a battle with food industry champions.

"We know from experiences in other countries that taxation on unhealthy food and drinks can improve health outcomes, and the strongest evidence of effectiveness is for a tax on sugar-sweetened beverages. If a tax of at least 20 % is introduced, it could reduce the prevalence of obesity in the UK by around 180,000 people," said Hollins.

"We know that the majority of the UK population, particularly low-income households, are not consuming enough fruit and vegetables, so financial measures should also be considered to subsidise their price, which has risen by 30 % since 2008. This is an important way to help redress the imbalance highlighted previously between the cost of healthy and unhealthy products, which particularly impacts on individuals and families affected by food poverty."

In 2011, David Cameron said the government was considering taxes on unhealthy foods, which would include those high in sugars, salt and saturated fats. But when the Life Sciences minister George Freeman raised the issue recently, he was slapped down. Asked in May if a sugar tax was being considered, the prime minister's spokesman said a definitive no. The government would be looking at other ways of tackling obesity, the spokesman said.

The government has chosen to address obesity through the voluntary responsibility deal with the food industry, which asks companies to make pledges on measures such as labelling and cutting calories in their packaged food products.

[...] The Food and Drink Federation said it shared the BMA's concerns about the health of young people, who needed "better, more balanced diets and lifestyles". But its director general, Ian Wright, added: "Many foods and drinks are already taxed at 20 %. Where additional taxes have been introduced they've not proven effective at driving long-term, lasting change to diets. We welcome Downing Street recently unequivocally ruling out a sugar tax and committing to a partnership approach to public health." *(529 words)*

Source: Sarah Boseley, on: www.theguardian.com, 13th July 2015

Editor's note: *Since April 2018, a tax on sugary drinks exists in the UK.*

Annotations

clampdown (l. 5): stopping, limitation; diet (l. 8): what sb usually eats and drinks; NHS (l. 10): short for "National Health Service", the publicly funded health care system of the UK; nutritional (l. 12): good for health and growth; champions (l. 18): *here:* leading firms; prevalence (l. 22): rate, number; (to) redress (l. 27): (to) correct, (to) set right; David Cameron (l. 30): British Prime Minister 2010–2016; (to) slap down (l. 33): (to) stop sb talking or making suggestions; unequivocally (l. 44): leaving no doubt

Basics

How to read the statistics on the next page

The statistics tell you how many adults in a million have died from consuming too many sugary drinks (this number is referred to as the "death rate concerning sugary drinks" in the respective country). However, the countries have been selected, which means that Germany does not rank ninth concerning deadly sugar consumption worldwide, for example.

The statistics show that in one year, **404.5 adults in Mexico** died as a result of drinking sugary drinks. However, if you think the calculation through for yourself, you have to know that the population of Mexico is actually about 120 million people and roughly 60 million of them are adults of the age of 18 and above. The total of 24,000 deaths is the result of multiplying 404.5 deaths (per 1 million adults) by 60 (overall number of adults in millions of people): **404.5 x 60 = 24,270**

In comparison, with about 65 million adults of the age of 18 and above in Germany, you need to multiply the figure of 49 deaths (per 1 million adults) by 65: **49 x 65 = 2,940**

Material: Statistics on death rate from sugary drinks

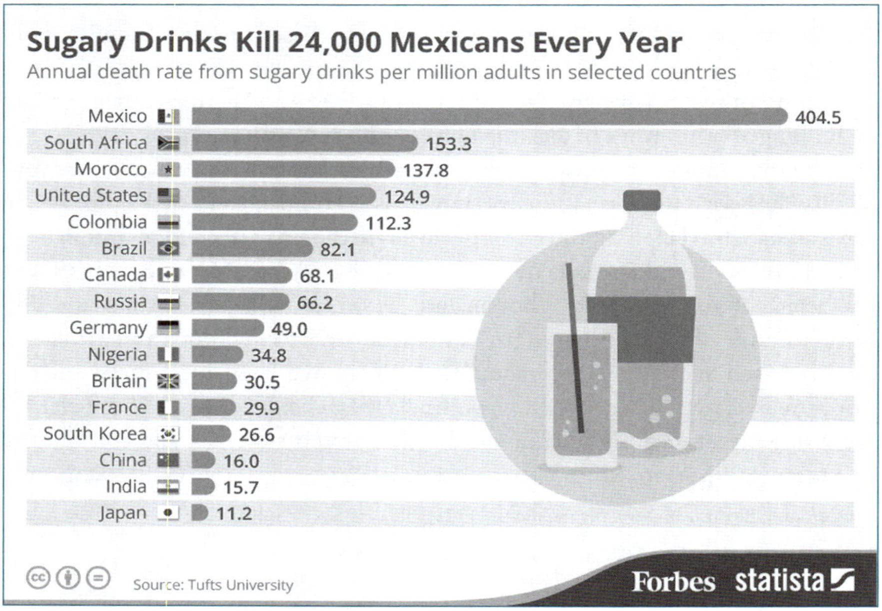

Source: Forbes/statista, licensed under CC-BY-ND-3.0

50 Im Rahmen eines Praktikums bei einer Krankenkasse werden Sie gebeten, einen Artikel für das Magazin „Jung & Fit" zu schreiben, das speziell für Versicherte unter 25 Jahren herausgegeben wird. Thema sollen Bemühungen gegen Fettleibigkeit bei Jugendlichen in Großbritannien sein. Als Grundlage für Ihren Artikel dienen Ihnen der Text „British doctors demand tax on sugary drinks" sowie die oben stehende Statistik.

a) Sammeln Sie zunächst Informationen zu den folgenden Leitfragen:
   - Was ist das Problem?
   - Welche Gründe bzw. Ursachen werden für das Problem genannt?
   - Was kann getan werden?

b) Verfassen Sie dann einen Artikel von etwa 250 Wörtern. Denken Sie daran, Ihren Text sinnvoll zu gliedern und ihn mit einer aussagekräftigen Überschrift zu versehen. Achten Sie ebenfalls darauf, einen für die Leserschaft des Magazins ansprechenden Text zu schreiben, der für einen verantwortungsvolleren Umgang mit der eigenen Gesundheit wirbt.

Tattoo removal is big business

A LONG AND COSTLY BUSINESS

By Victoria Lambert

[...] [W]hat seemed like a good idea at the time may later be a cause for remorse: almost a third of those who have tattoos live to regret their body art, according to a survey from the British Association of Dermatologists. Thankfully, tattoos are not as permanent as they used to be. [...]

Rebecca Smail, a 24 year-old PR from London, was just 16 when she opted for an ankle tattoo – a "weird symbol in black, green and purple" which she chose from a book on the subject.

"Initially I was pleased," she says. "It cost about £ 50 at a tattooist in Exeter and took about 45 minutes to complete. But over the past five years, I've come to find it embarrassing. I'm fed up with people asking what it means – because I don't know. And I understand for older generations, there are negative connotations to tattoos. My parents weren't particularly happy."

Rebecca opted to have her tattoo removed by laser, a technique now being offered by an increasing number of high street dermatology clinics. It works by using powerful beams of coloured laser light to turn the ink, using heat, into tiny particles. Red and green lights are good for breaking down, respectively, black, brown and dark shades of green and blue, and red, purple and orange colours. The particles are then absorbed into the body via the bloodstream, and excreted via the liver and digestive system.

Lasering is a lengthy, expensive procedure – costs vary but the average is about £ 200 a session, with the number of sessions needed depending on the size and colour. Nor is it ever guaranteed to totally remove a tattoo. [...] [S]ome people will always be left with "ghosting" – a shadowy outline – depending on the size and colour of the original design; and [...] lasers do not yet exist (although they are in development) which will remove certain blues or light greens, or pale colours like yellow or pink. Nor are lasers recommended for darker skins, as there is a risk the laser will strip out natural pigmentation and leave white scarring. [...]

Claims are also being made for an alternative therapy in which special liquid is injected into the tattoo, just as the ink was initially. The liquid is said to bond with the colour pigments, and both are then broken down and excreted by the body, leaving a scab behind which should heal normally. The treatment is cheaper than laser but Stuart Harrison, the director of Oxford Skin Clinics, which offers this treatment, admits that it isn't suitable for old, deep or overly large tattoos. "It would end up being very expensive and removal could take years," he says.

Tattoo removal is rarely carried out on the NHS. Prof Harry Moseley, head of the Department of Plastic Surgery at Ninewells Hospital and Medical School, Dundee and head of the British Medical Laser Association, says: "At our NHS clinic we do carry out tattoo removal but only in a small number of cases where the patient is severely distressed." [...]

Surgical excision is not new, is no cheaper than laser therapy (an average tattoo might cost between £850–£1,400 to remove), and ultimately takes as long. However, being carried out under local anaesthetic, it is painless and the tattoo is guaranteed to be removed completely. [...]

[Plastic surgeon Paul Banwell, whose private cosmetic surgery clinic offers surgical removal of tattoos,] says: "There are limitations to surgical removal; it wouldn't work for large tattoos or where the skin is naturally taut, or where the whole of a limb is affected such as a tattoo 'sleeve' on the arm. The only way to get rid of a large tattoo by excision would be to treat it like a tumour removal or burn treatment, so that means cutting out all the affected skin, and then using a graft to repair the hole." *(651 words)*

Source: Victoria Lambert, on: www.telegraph.co.uk, 12th January 2015

Annotations

remorse (ll. 1/2): regret; connotation to (ll. 11/12): association with; particle (l. 16): a tiny part of sth; liver (l. 19): *Leber*; digestive system (l. 19): *Verdauung*; NHS (l. 37): short for "National Health Service", the publicly funded health care system of the United Kingdom; taut (l. 48): stretched; graft (l. 52): transplant

51 Die ältere Schwester Ihrer Freundin hat sich als Teenager ein Tattoo stechen lassen. Jetzt will sie sich beruflich umorientieren und strebt eine Ausbildung zur Bankkauffrau an. Da sie im Rahmen ihrer Lehre oft Kontakt mit Kunden haben wird, ist eine Tätowierung in diesem Berufsfeld nicht gern gesehen. Daher sucht sie nach Möglichkeiten, das Tattoo loszuwerden. Im Englischunterricht haben Sie den oben stehenden Artikel behandelt und glauben, dass er für die Schwester Ihrer Freundin interessant sein könnte.

a) Vervollständigen Sie die folgende Tabelle mit Informationen zu den unterschiedlichen Möglichkeiten, sich ein Tattoo entfernen zu lassen.

	Vorteile	**Nachteile**
Laser-technologie		
Injektion einer Flüssigkeit		
Chirurgischer Eingriff		

b) Schreiben Sie aufbauend auf den gesammelten Informationen der Schwester Ihrer Freundin eine E-Mail von etwa 200 Wörtern, in der Sie ihr die entsprechenden Möglichkeiten aufzeigen.

The generation gap

An election manifesto aimed at helping young people and their money could prove popular among parents, suggests KATIE MORLEY.

The future for young people in Britain is precarious – more so than we are too often led to believe. We are a nation deep in debt, and the comfortable quality of life to which older generations have become accustomed, looks increasingly unaffordable for their offspring.

People in their 20s and 30s aspire to their parents' level of financial security – but are not on track to achieve it. For some it first dawns when they graduate from university with £45,000 of debt, are unable to get a "graduate" job and are forced to accept bar work instead. It hits them again when they crave adult independence in their 20s but are paid so little they can't afford to move out of their childhood bedroom. And when they consider having children of their own, but can only afford a one-bedroom flat to raise them in, that's when they know that something's not right. [...]

My generation is accused of being apathetic but there is a stirring unrest among those of us trying – and struggling – to build financial security. One of the biggest concerns ought to be the growing national debt that stretches further into the future than most of us care to imagine. This terrifying bill, much of which derives from promised spending on state pensions and benefits for older generations, will end up being footed by today's young people. This is despite them being told that by the time they themselves come to retire, the public purse will not afford them anywhere near as generous state funded income – if anything at all.

Those older generations – I mean those in the 50s, 60s, and 70s – seem oblivious to the problems they may be creating for those in future. A quick glance at the financial security they have enjoyed unchallenged for years, could explain why. According to Joseph Rowntree Foundation data the average pensioner now earns more than the average working person. Even so, the Government chooses to lavish them with an array of exclusive tax-funded perks such as free bus passes, pensioner bonds, generous state pensions and tax relief on investments they are more than other generations likely to own – such as buy-to-let properties. Older generations have an innate sense of comfort and security thanks to the property wealth they have accumulated. Some believe they have earned this money. In truth, housing values have risen largely because of consistent undersupply. For older people to realise the value of their homes they are also relying on younger generations stretching themselves to the brink with enormous mortgages.

[...] Because of boomers' enormous voting power, political parties strive to maintain the status quo. To them, the next four years matter more than anything else, so they continue to dish out sweeteners even though they know they will harm our country in the long run. By doing this our leaders are irresponsibly creating the impression that we can afford to preserve older people's perks. All this could not be further from reality. [...]

Politicians should be bold enough to admit this. They should lift young people's bleak trajectory with a manifesto which aims to distribute wealth more fairly across generations, and reduce national debt.

It is obvious that young people would be more likely to vote for such policies. But as this newspaper has already pointed out, their numbers are so small that increased ballot action among 18-24s would be futile in ending the political dominance of the old. But it strikes me that genuine policies of this nature would also give older voters fresh impetus to vote. Faced with a chance to choose a set of policies designed to genuinely help their offspring, what parent would not vote to protect the interests of their child? [...] It is time to stop protecting the baby boomers from the truth – and let them prove – that they are not a selfish generation. *(646 words)*

Source: Katie Morley, on: www.telegraph.co.uk, 26th February 2015

Annotations

manifesto (introduction): programme; precarious (l. 1): insecure; (to) derive from sth (l. 17): (to) stem from sth; (to) be footed by (l. 18): (to) be paid by; (to) be oblivious to sth (l. 23): (to) not be aware of sth; (to) lavish sb with sth (l. 27): (to) shower sb with sth; array (l. 27): collection, number; perk (l. 27): benefit; innate (l. 30): natural; mortgage (l. 35): *Hypothek (auf eine Immobilie)*; (baby) boomers (ll. 36, 52): a generation with a high birth rate, usually born after the nation was facing a tough time such as a war etc.; bold (l. 42): brave; trajectory (l. 43): *here:* prospect

52 Sie haben den obigen Artikel zufällig auf der Homepage einer englischen Zeitung entdeckt, als Sie eine Internetrecherche zum Thema „Inherent problems of modern British society" für den Englischunterricht durchgeführt haben. Aus Interesse lesen Sie sich den Artikel durch und sind über seinen Inhalt entsetzt. Da Sie sich ernsthaft Sorgen machen, dass sich auch Deutschland in eine ähnliche Richtung entwickelt, beschließen Sie, einen Brief an Ihre(n) Bundestagsabgeordnete(n) zu verfassen, in dem Sie die Situation junger Leute in Großbritannien darlegen, so wie sie sich im Artikel darstellt.

a) Um alle wichtigen Informationen zusammenzutragen, bitten Sie Ihren Bruder, der Anglistik studiert, den Artikel zusammenzufassen. Leider hat er eine sehr schwer zu lesende Handschrift, und es gelingt Ihnen nicht, einzelne Wörter zu entziffern. Folglich müssen Sie den Artikel noch einmal lesen, um die Lücken im Text zu füllen.

Junge Briten zwischen 20 und 30 Jahren dürfen nicht hoffen, denselben hohen ____________ zu erreichen wie ihre Eltern und Großeltern. Nach Abschluss ihres Studiums stehen junge Erwachsene oft vor erheblichen Problemen. Aufgrund hoher ____________ in Großbritannien haben sie einen Berg Schulden und oft ist es Ihnen nicht möglich, eine ____________ zu finden, die ihrer ____________ entspricht. In schlecht bezahlten Jobs ist aber der ____________ häufig nicht hoch genug, um sich eine eigene ____________ oder gar die Gründung einer ____________ leisten zu können. Zu all diesen Belastungen kommt aber noch die Tatsache, dass junge Menschen für die ____________ der Rentner und Pensionäre aufkommen müssen. Allein die Rente der Babyboomer-Generation liegt oft deutlich über dem ____________ vieler Arbeitnehmer. Auch werden Rentnern oft ____________ wie verbilligte ____________ im öffentlichen Nahverkehr und Steuerentlastungen angeboten. Durch die Wohnungsknappheit gewinnen zudem ihre ____________ an Wert, was aber auch dazu führt, dass junge Menschen sie sich nicht leisten können. Aus Angst vor dem Verlust von ____________ verschließen ____________ die Augen vor dieser Entwicklung. Dabei wären auch viele ältere Wähler bereit, für die Zukunft ihrer Kinder und Enkel ____________ zu akzeptieren, um die finanzielle Lage des Landes zu ____________, wenn es ein vernünftiges ____________ zur Verteilung der ____________ auf alle Generationen gibt.

b) Schreiben Sie einen Brief an Ihre(n) Abgeordnete(n). Appellieren Sie an sie (ihn), die Startchancen für junge Menschen in Deutschland zu verbessern, wo eine ähnlich schwierige Situation wie in Großbritannien besteht. Ihr Schreiben sollte ungefähr 250 Wörter umfassen.

Language in Use: Grammar

Adjectives and adverbs

Basics

Unterscheidung Adjektiv – Adverb

Stellung im Satz

- Das **Adjektiv** steht bei einem **Substantiv** oder einem **Pronomen** und bestimmt es näher.
- Das **Adverb** bestimmt ein **Verb** oder ein **Adjektiv** genauer.

More than 100 million years ago different kinds of dinosaurs lived on our earth.
They were too slow to react to changes.

The process in which animals change slowly is called evolution. Darwin showed that no two animals were exactly alike.

Comparison of adjectives

Comparison with *-er/-est*

Für alle einsilbigen und für die zweisilbigen Adjektive, die auf *-y*, *-le*, *-ow* oder *-er* enden.

Grundform	Komparativ	Superlativ
fast	faster	fastest
easy	easier	easiest
simple	simpler	simplest
narrow	narrower	narrowest
clever	cleverer	cleverest

Comparison with *more/most*

Für die meisten zweisilbigen und alle mehrsilbigen Adjektive.

Grundform	Komparativ	Superlativ
famous	more famous	most famous
interesting	more interesting	most interesting

Irregular comparison

Grundform	Komparativ	Superlativ
bad	worse	worst
good	better	best
late	later	latest (*„das neueste“*)/last (*bei Reihen*)
little (= *wenig*)	less	least
little (= *klein*)	littler	littlest
much/many (= *viel/viele*)	more	most
near	nearer	nearest (*bei Entfernungen*) next (*bei Reihen*)
far	farther/further	farthest/furthest

Comparison of adverbs

Bei den Adverbien gibt es wie bei den Adjektiven zwei Formen der Steigerung.

Comparison with *more/most*

Für alle auf *-ly* endenden Adverbien.

Grundform	Komparativ	Superlativ
easily	more easily	most easily
quickly	more quickly	most quickly

Comparison with *-er/-est*

Für Adverbien, die die gleiche Form haben wie das jeweilige Adjektiv, am gebräuchlichsten sind: *fast, early, hard, late, long, near, high, low* und *soon.*

Grundform	Komparativ	Superlativ
early	earlier	earliest
soon	sooner	soonest

Irregular comparison

Wird das zugehörige Adjektiv unregelmäßig gesteigert, gilt dies auch für das Adverb.

Grundform	Komparativ	Superlativ
bad	worse	worst
well	better	best

Adjective or adverb?

Nach diesen Verben steht das Adjektiv (nicht das Adverb)

- to become, to get, to grow, to keep, to look (= *aussehen*), to remain, to seem — All the boys remained quiet.
- to smell, to sound, to taste — Their latest CD sounds great.

Adverbien mit unterschiedlichen Formen und Bedeutungen

fair	*gerecht*	fairly	*ziemlich*
hard	*schwer*	hardly	*kaum*
high	*hoch*	highly	*sehr*
just	*gerade*	justly	*zu Recht*
late	*spät*	lately	*kürzlich, in letzter Zeit*
near	*nahe*	nearly	*beinahe*

53 Use the comparative or superlative form of the adjective or adverb in brackets.

The ______________ *(recent)* discovery of human bone fragments in Africa is a scientific sensation. The bones which were discovered in Ethiopia are 500,000 years ________________ *(old)* than any human remains found before. These fossils represent our ______________ *(old)* direct human ancestors. With these bones scientists will be able to carry out the ___________________ *(detailed)* investigation into the origins of man and ideas about how our ancestors lived. The ___________________ *(fascinating)* aspect of the discovery are the 20 teeth which were excavated. The findings suggest that those humans were ______________ *(likely)* vegetarians. Remains of plants and seeds were found _________________ *(frequently)* with the skeletons than bones of animals. That is why it is _____________ *(likely)* that they ate plants and fruit than that they hunted animals. They ________________ *(certainly)* made no stone tools.

54 Decide whether to use adjectives or adverbs in these sentences.

Shirley Binghall works as a conservator in the British Museum. Her job is to keep the ________________ *(valuable)* objects in ______________ *(good)* condition so that they look ________________ *(beautiful)* when they are displayed ________________ *(public)*. Because of her ______________ *(extreme)* ___________ *(long)* experience Shirley knows ________________ *(exact)* how to look after the artefacts ______________ *(proper)*. Last week she was given an _______________ *(exceptional)* _____________ *(difficult)* job. German archaeologists in Troy had ________________ *(careful)* unearthed ______________ *(numerous)* pieces of a pot that was ________________ *(probable)* Greek. Although the dirty-brown pieces looked ___________ *(fair)* ______________ *(worthless)* at first sight, Shirley knew ________________ *(immediate)* that the Germans had found a _____________ *(real)* beauty. Shirley ______________ *(careful)* placed all the pieces on her working table. There they look ________________ *(just)* like a jigsaw puzzle. Then Shirley ______________ *(cautious)* cleaned the pieces and tried to fit them together. For several days she worked ______________ *(regular)* on repairing the object. Using sellotape, plaster and wax, Shirley ______________ *(final)* succeeded in sticking the pieces into place. Although several pieces were missing, she didn't find it ______________ *(hard)* to date the pot ______________ *(correct)*. She ______________ *(hard)* ever tries to paint over the missing pieces, in order to give the visitors a ______________ *(clear)* picture of which parts are old and which have ______________ *(recent)* been added.

The tenses

Basics

Das Aktiv

Simple or progressive

Tenses	Simple Form	Progressive Form
Present	I do	I'm doing
Future I	I'll do	I'll be doing
Future II	I'll have done	
Past	I did	I was doing
Present Perfect	I have done	I have been doing
Past Perfect	I had done	I had been doing
Conditional I	I would do	
Conditional II	I would have done	

Choosing the right tense

Talking about the future

Tenses	Usage	Example
Present tense	*Etwas geschieht häufiger oder ist allgemein wahr.*	Scotland is famous for its beautiful lakes and romantic castles.
Future tense	*Etwas wird geschehen.*	New reports of an alleged sighting of a monster will attract more tourists.
Past tense	*Eine Handlung ist abgeschlossen.*	In 1934 a newspaper published a photo of the "Loch Ness monster".
Present perfect	*Eine Handlung oder ein Zustand der Vergangenheit hat einen Bezug zur Gegenwart.*	People have always been interested in legends and mysteries.
Past perfect	*Zwei Handlungen, die beide in der Vergangenheit liegen, werden in die richtige Reihenfolge gebracht.*	After the scientists had explored the lake for several weeks, they gave up the search for the monster.

Present perfect or simple past

Tenses: Simple past – present perfect

Eine besondere Lernschwierigkeit stellt die richtige Verwendung des **present perfect** dar, da es im Deutschen keine Entsprechung dazu gibt. Es ist relativ gleichgültig, ob man sagt „Gestern las ich ein interessantes Buch" (= Präteritum / Imperfekt) oder „Gestern habe ich ein interessantes Buch gelesen" (= Perfekt).

Uns ist klar, dass beide Vorgänge vergangen sind. Im Englischen können Handlungen, die in der Vergangenheit begonnen haben und in der Vergangenheit beendet wurden, nur im **simple past** wiedergegeben werden. Die Verwendung des **present perfect** ist eng an eine bestimmte Aussageabsicht geknüpft.

Simple past

Im *simple past* werden Handlungen wiedergegeben, die in der **Vergangenheit begannen und abgeschlossen** wurden. Es ist die **typische Zeitform** für **Erzählungen** und **Berichte**. Signalwörter: *ago, in 1934, in AD 565, last week/month/year, yesterday, then* etc.	In 1934 Colonel Robert Wilson took a picture of the Loch Ness monster. *1934 fotografierte Robert Wilson das Monster von Loch Ness.*

Present perfect

Das *present perfect* drückt aus, dass eine **Handlung in der Vergangenheit begonnen hat** und einen **Bezug zur Gegenwart** besitzt. Signalwörter: *all year long, ever, for, since*	Since 1933 more than 3,000 people have claimed to have seen the "monster". *Seit 1933 haben über 3.000 Menschen behauptet, das „Monster" gesehen zu haben.*

55 Put the verbs in brackets into the correct tense.

a) Hey Jeff, ________________ *(you/ever/be)* to Scotland?

b) Yes, I ________________ *(go)* there last year with my parents.

c) While you ________________ *(drive)* along the lake, ________________ *(you/observe)* anything mysterious?

d) No, I ________________ *(not, see)* the monster then if that's what you mean. But when we ________________ *(go)* into the museum I ________________ *(look at)* a giant-size model of Nessie.

e) For more than sixty years people ________________ *(claim)* that they ________________ *(see)* "Nessie". In 1934 one even ________________ *(say)* he had taken a picture! But now, it ________________ *(prove/just)* that the photo was a fake.

f) I ________________ *(never/believe)* in that legend anyway!

56 Choose the correct form of the verb in brackets.

Hotel directors, castle owners and tourist managers ____________ *(are always trying/always try)* to think of new ways of attracting more guests and visitors. Many ____________ *(have even played/have even been playing)* with the idea of inventing a spectacular ghost or monster, such as Nessie. The legendary creature which is supposed ____________ *(to live/to be living)* in Loch Ness ____________ *(is still arousing/still arouses)* the interest of tourists. For decades Nessie ____________ *(has drawn/has been drawing)* large numbers of visitors to the lonely lake in the Scottish Highlands.

The Argentinian version of Nessie ____________ *(is being called/is called)* Nahuelito. Local Indians maintain that a monster ____________ *(has lived/has been living)* in the Nahuel Huapi Lake since ancient times. The lake, which ____________ *(is covering/covers)* 318 square miles, ____________ *(is lying/lies)* at the foot of the Patagonian mountains. At present, plans ____________ *(are discussed/are being discussed)* to build a visitor centre. Scores of tourists are convinced that they have seen a huge snake-like creature in the water while they ____________ *(drove/were driving)* along the shores of the lake. In bars and restaurants in Bariloche you can listen to visitors who ____________ *(tell/are telling)* stories about their sightings. One of them said he ____________ *(sat/was sitting)* on the edge of the lake fishing when suddenly a hump ____________ *(was appearing/appeared)* from under the surface. In spite of reports like this one, there are still many people who ____________ *(are not believing/do not believe)* in monsters or ghosts.

57 Supply the correct tense of the verbs in brackets.

About five years ago I ______________ *(travel)* to Scotland for the first time and ______________ *(fascinate)* immediately by the beautiful landscape, the romantic castles and the historic sites. It ______________ *(rain)* almost every day when I ______________ *(explore)* the Highlands, but that ______________ *(not worry)* me as friends who ______________ *(be)* to Scotland before ______________ *(warn)* me. I ______________ *(not able)* to go hiking on my first trip so I ______________ *(decide)* to come back as soon as possible. Two years later, I ______________ *(persuade)* my friends Simon and Marc to accompany me on a rambling tour through the Grampians. Both ______________ *(love)* the Highlands because they ______________ *(visit)* Scotland when they ______________ *(be)* teenagers but ______________ *(not be)* back since. Early summer ______________ *(be)* a good season for hiking, so Marc, Simon and I ______________ *(set out)* on another trip to Scotland next June. We ______________ *(must save)* a lot of money to buy our camping equipment. We ______________ *(buy)* our flight tickets soon because I'm afraid prices ______________ *(go)* up again before the summer season starts. I'm sure we ______________ *(enjoy)* our tour and that this ______________ *(not be)* my last visit to that beautiful country.

Active and passive voice

Basics

Das Passiv

Bildung

Das Passiv wird gebildet mit einer Form von ***to be* + Partizip Perfekt**.

Tense	Active Voice	Passive Voice
Present	The film star signs the contract.	The contract is signed by the film star.
Past	The film star signed the contract yesterday.	The contract was signed by the film star yesterday.
Present perfect	The film star has signed the contract already.	The contract has already been signed by the film star.
Past perfect	The film star had signed the contract before.	The contract had been signed by the film star before.
Future I	The film star will sign the contract next month.	The contract will be signed by the film star next month.
Future II	The film star will have signed the contract before long.	The contract will have been signed by the film star before long.
Conditional I	The film star would sign the contract if …	The contract would be signed by the film star if …
Conditional II	The film star would have signed the contract if …	The contract would have been signed by the film star if …

Passive progressive

Die Verlaufsform des Passivs wird gebildet mit ***to be* + *being* + Partizip Perfekt**.
Hier gibt es nur die Formen *present progressive* und *past progressive*.

Tense	Active Voice	Passive Voice
Present	The BBC is televising the Oscar ceremony.	The Oscar ceremony is being televised by the BBC. *Die Oscarfeier wird (gerade) von der BBC übertragen.*
Past	The BBC was televising the Oscar ceremony.	The Oscar ceremony was being televised by the BBC. *Die Oscarfeier wurde (über eine längere Zeit) von der BBC übertragen.*

58 Put these sentences into passive voice.

Example:

Active Voice	Passive Voice
James Cook chose him as his navigator.	He was chosen as navigator by James Cook.

a) The plantation owners use the bread fruit trees as a cheap source of food.

____

b) All his friends will ask him to join.

____

c) Fletcher respected the older man for his abilities as a seaman.

____

d) The old sailor is teaching his son how to draw a chart.

____

e) The lazy sailors did not obey orders.

____

f) The mutineers had burnt the ship.

____

g) We regard Bligh's voyage as a masterpiece in navigation.

h) He lost seven of his 18 men.

i) In 1817 they buried him in London.

j) Two American writers have used the story for a novel.

k) The MGM film company is still making a profit with the film on the mutiny.

59 Remember the old Egyptians? They developed the strange art of embalming their deceased. The following text tells you about the method they used. It may sound a bit crude in places, but this is how it really worked.

Put these sentences into active voice.
Use "the Egyptian embalmers" (or "they") as the subject of the sentences.

a) All the organs were taken out and preserved separately.

b) Only the heart was left in place.

c) The brain was drawn out of the head through the nose.

d) The body was cleaned and filled with spices and herbs.

e) Bags of white powder, natron, were used to dry the body.

f) Finally it was wrapped in many layers of linen bandages.

g) A mask was put over the face.

h) The body was then put into a coffin.

i) Several coffins were used to protect the mummy.

Relative clauses

Basics

Notwendige und nicht-notwendige Relativsätze

Das Relativpronomen / *Relative Pronouns*

• Ein Relativsatz bezieht sich auf eine im Hauptsatz genannte Person oder Sache und bestimmt oder beschreibt sie näher. Das Relativpronomen für Personen ist *who*, für Dinge *which*.	My best friend is the only person who always knows how to cheer me up. My best friend always tells me jokes which make me laugh.

Notwendige (*defining*) und nicht-notwendige (*non-defining*) Relativsätze

• *Defining relative clauses* bestimmen das Bezugswort näher und sind zum richtigen Verständnis des Satzes erforderlich. Der Relativsatz wird **nicht** durch Kommas abgetrennt. Das Relativpronomen kann weggelassen werden, wenn es das **Objekt** des Satzes ist (*contact clause*).	I don't know who to ask for help. This is a topic which I have always tried to avoid. The pupil whose job it is to clean the board is ill today. Mrs Carter is a teacher (who/that) I cannot stand. Pizza is the dish (that/which) I like best.
• *Non-defining relative clauses* werden eher im schriftlichen Englisch verwendet. Der Relativsatz wird hier durch **Kommas** vom Hauptsatz abgetrennt. Die Information im Relativsatz ist zum Verständnis des Hauptsatzes **nicht notwendig**.	My aunt Jessica, who works as an engineer, has just got promoted. *Animal Farm*, which is my favourite book, was written by George Orwell. My friend Amy, whose jokes always make me laugh, is a very funny person.

Verwendung von *that, whom, which, what*

• *That* wird nur in notwendigen Relativsätzen verwendet.	My best friend always tells me jokes that make me laugh.
• *Whom* kann statt *who* für das Objekt des Relativsatzes verwendet werden.	This is the famous actor whom I was dying to meet.
• *Which* wird gebraucht, wenn sich der Relativsatz auf den gesamten Inhalt des vorhergehenden Satzes bezieht.	Amy always speaks her mind, which can be pretty embarrassing sometimes.
• *What* wird gebraucht, wenn sich der Relativsatz auf den gesamten Inhalt des folgenden Satzes bezieht.	I'm sorry I can't go to the cinema with you tonight. I have a lot of homework to do, and what's even worse, a very bad cold as well.

60 Put in relative pronouns where necessary.

In November 2013, Prince Harry joined one of three teams ______________ aim it was to trek more than 200 miles to the South Pole. The teams consisted of servicemen and -women from the UK and other nations, ______________ had suffered terrible war injuries. The prince, ______________ was patron of the expedition, belonged to Team UK, ______________ included four injured British soldiers. Due to the extreme weather conditions the expedition teams were followed by a support team, ______________ were on hand in case of emergencies. The adventure, ______________ lasted for more than three weeks, was successfully completed on December 13, 2013. Ed Parker, the director ______________ led the expedition, said, "We always knew that this wasn't going to be easy, but we were determined to get 12 men and women, all injured in conflict, to the South Pole".

Reaching the South Pole was not the only purpose ____________ the organisers had in mind; in fact, what was more important was to raise money for military charities.

Harry, ______________ after his father, his brother and the latter's children is next in line to the throne, is the first member of the Royal Family to trek to the geographic South Pole. In the past, he had sometimes been the subject of reports ______________ wanted to show him as a careless party-goer. However, the prince has dedicated a lot of his time working for a good cause. The expedition to the South Pole was not the first charity work ______________ Harry has taken part in. He was a member of the charity's trek ______________ headed to the North Pole in 2011. ______________ kept him from completing the expedition then was his brother's wedding, ______________ he had to attend.

61 Combine the following pairs of sentences by means of relative pronouns. Make any changes necessary concerning word order and structure to do so.

a) There is a triangle in the Atlantic Ocean. One corner is the island of Bermuda.

b) The Triangle is a vast stretch of open sea. It covers more than 1 million square miles.

c) In 1945 the crews of five torpedo bombers were lost over the Bermuda Triangle. They had been on a training flight.

d) In September 1950 an article was published in the *Miami Herald*. It reported the unusual disappearances of several ships and planes.

e) Over the years more planes and ships made the headlines. Their disappearance could not be explained.

f) **Numerous theories have been put forward about the mysterious disappearances. None of them is convincing.**

____

____

g) **Hollywood producers made several films and TV series about the Bermuda Triangle. They were sure the subject would interest people.**

____

____

62 Make sentences with relative pronouns. Leave out the pronoun where possible (contact clause).

a) I will never forget the film *Avatar*, ____________ I saw when I was twelve.

b) The science fiction film tells a story ____________ set on a planet in the distant future.

c) The action takes place on the moon Pandora, ____________ atmosphere is poisonous to humans.

d) Pandora is inhabited by blue-skinned humanoids ____________ live in harmony with nature.

e) The director of the film was James Cameron, ____________ had made the box-office hit *Titanic*.

f) The money ____________ Cameron had earned with *Titanic* was invested in the development of *Avatar*.

g) *Avatar* made use of actors ____________ had been generated by computers.

h) It contains everything ____________ cinema-goers could wish for.

i) The movie, ____________ won three Oscars, became the most profitable film of all time.

Conditional clauses

Conditional sentences

Basics

Bedingungssätze

In Konditionalsätzen drückt man eine Bedingung aus. Wir unterscheiden die beiden Satzteile Bedingungssatz *(if-clause)* und Hauptsatz *(main clause)*. Im Englischen gibt es unterschiedliche Bedingungssätze, die eine bestimmte Zeitenfolge in Haupt- und Bedingungssatz erfordern.

Probable condition (Typ 1: Erfüllbare Bedingung)

Im *if*-Satz steht eine Bedingung, die der Sprecher / die Sprecherin für erfüllbar hält. Wenn im ***if*-Satz** das **Präsens** verwendet wird, steht im **Hauptsatz** das **Futur I**.

if-clause	main clause
If you train hard, *Wenn ihr fleißig trainiert,*	you will become good athletes. *werdet ihr gute Sportler*innen (werden).*

Improbable condition (Typ 2: Unwahrscheinliche Bedingung)

Im *if*-Satz steht eine Bedingung, deren Erfüllung der Sprecher / die Sprecherin für eher unwahrscheinlich hält. Wenn im ***if*-Satz** das **Präteritum** steht, folgt im **Hauptsatz Konditional I**. Bei diesem Typ wird *was* im *if*-Satz meistens zu *were* („*subjunctive*").

if-clause	main clause
If you got an invitation from NASA, *Wenn du eine Einladung von der NASA bekämest (bekommen würdest),*	would you like to fly into space? *würdest du gerne in den Weltraum fliegen?*
If I were rich, *Wenn ich reich wäre,*	I would buy a ticket for a flight into space. *würde ich ein Ticket für einen Flug ins Weltall kaufen.*

Impossible condition (Typ 3: Unmögliche Bedingung)

Im *if*-Satz steht eine Bedingung, die nicht mehr erfüllt werden kann, da sich der Satz auf die Vergangenheit bezieht. Damit stellt diese Bedingung eine bloße Annahme dar. Wenn im ***if*-Satz** das **Plusquamperfekt** steht, folgt im **Hauptsatz Konditional II**.

if-clause	main clause
If astronauts had not brought back rock samples from the moon,	scientists would have been disappointed.

63 Supply the missing forms.

a) If there ____________ *(not, be)* any gravity, things would float around in the air.

b) Things ____________ *(not, fall)* to the ground if there wasn't any gravity.

c) Astronauts ______________ *(not, can, survive)* in space if they didn't wear space suits.

d) Astronauts couldn't have walked on the moon if they ______________ *(not, wear)* space suits.

e) If we travelled at the speed of light, we ______________ *(can, visit)* other planets.

f) We could visit other planets if they ______________ *(not, be)* so far away.

g) If the astronauts didn't do any exercise during their flights, their muscles ______________ *(get)* weak because of weightlessness.

h) If satellites ______________ *(not, have)* solar panels, they wouldn't have any energy for their instruments.

i) Weather forecasts ______________ *(be)* more precise years ago if meteorologists had had weather satellites earlier.

j) If there weren't any TV satellites in space, live broadcasts from other continents ______________ *(not, be)* possible.

k) TV satellites wouldn't stay above the same place all the time if they ______________ *(not, move)* in time with the Earth.

64 Choose the correct grammatical form and mark it with a cross (✗).

a) If everything goes according to plan, the Space Agency ...

- ☐ presented a number of spectacular space projects soon.
- ☐ would present a number of spectacular space projects soon.
- ☐ will present a number of spectacular space projects soon.

b) A robot to Mars could be launched soon if funds ...

- ☐ were available in time.
- ☐ are available in time.
- ☐ will be available in time.

c) Sending probes into space would be cheaper if weight …
- ☐ isn't such a big problem.
- ☐ wasn't such a big problem.
- ☐ would not be such a big problem.

d) If engineers knew more about suitable landing sites, spacecrafts …
- ☐ could be landed more safely.
- ☐ would have been landed more safely.
- ☐ would have landed more safely.

e) If the solar panels had unfolded properly, the robot …
- ☐ could drill into the Martian soil for a longer period.
- ☐ could have drilled into the Martian soil for a longer period.
- ☐ can drill into the Martian soil for a longer period.

f) The government would supply more funds if the general public …
- ☐ supports space exploration more enthusiastically.
- ☐ supported space exploration more enthusiastically.
- ☐ will support space exploration more enthusiastically.

g) If NASA had not been so successful in the past, funds …
- ☐ would have been cut.
- ☐ will be cut.
- ☐ were cut.

h) If science fiction authors were right, time travel …
- ☐ is easy.
- ☐ would be easy.
- ☐ could have been possible.

i) If mission control loses contact, the robot …
- ☐ would not have been able to explore more sites.
- ☐ would not be able to explore more sites.
- ☐ will not be able to explore more sites.

Modal auxiliaries

Basics

Die Besonderheiten der modalen Hilfsverben

Verben im Englischen können sein: Vollverben, die Verben *be, do, have* (Voll- oder Hilfsverben), und Hilfsverben, die nie alleine stehen können. Die modalen Hilfsverben *(can, could, may, might, must, shall, should, will, would)* bilden eine Sondergruppe innerhalb der Hilfsverben.

Modale Hilfsverben

• **Eine Form** für alle Personen (kein *-s* in der 3. Person Singular).	He must help her. We must help our friends.
• Der **Infinitiv** folgt **ohne *to***.	You must work more.
• **Frage** und **Verneinung** werden ohne *do/does/did* gebildet.	Can I help you?
Dabei drückt ***must not*** *(mustn't)* ein Verbot aus.	Arthur mustn't keep the book forever. *Artus darf das Buch nicht für immer behalten.*
Need not *(needn't)* drückt das Fehlen eines Zwangs oder einer Notwendigkeit aus. Es kann auch durch *does not have to* ersetzt werden.	But he needn't return it immediately. *(= But he doesn't have to …)* Aber er braucht es nicht sofort zurückzugeben.
• In bestimmten Zeitformen (Futur, Perfekt, Plusquamperfekt) wird statt des modalen Hilfsverbs ein **Ersatzverb** *(substitute)* verwendet.	We must take a test today. *Wir müssen heute eine Prüfung machen.* We will have to take a test soon. *Wir werden bald eine Prüfung machen müssen.*

Survey: "can" in all tenses

Tenses	Positive forms	Negative forms
Present	I can fight	I can't/cannot fight
Future	I'll be able to fight	I won't be able to fight
Past	I could/was able to fight	I couldn't/wasn't able to fight
Present Perfect	I have been able to fight	I haven't been able to fight
Past Perfect	I had been able to fight	I hadn't been able to fight
Conditional I	I could/would be able to fight	I couldn't/wouldn't be able to fight
Conditional II	I could have fought I would have been able to fight	I couldn't have fought I wouldn't have been able to fight

Survey: Substitutes

Modal	Substitute	Modal	Substitute
can *(können)*	to be able to	shall *(sollen)*	to be to
may *(dürfen)*	to be allowed to	will *(wollen)*	to want/wish/desire
must *(müssen)*	to have to		

65 Supply the correct form of the modal auxiliaries and verbs in brackets.

He ________________ *(must, regard)* as a typical example of the video game generation. When he was young Daniel just ________________ *(can, not, get)* enough of ghost stories and fairy tales about gnomes and wizards. His mother ________________ *(must, not, call)* him twice when it was time for a bedtime story. No wonder Daniel ________________ *(can, hardly, wait)* until he was bought his first computer and computer games. Although he ________________ *(may, only, play)* after he had finished his homework, his mother often ________________ *(must, remind)* him to stop gaming and go out for a change. On Saturdays Daniel ________________ *(can, not, play)*, because he worked in a supermarket to earn extra pocket money so that he ________________ *(can, afford)* to buy more games. He ________________ *(need, not, spend)* too much as he ________________ *(can, share)* costs with his friend Jason, another online game addict. Sometimes they joined a LAN party, where they ________________ *(can, play)* for hours. Last month Daniel took his final exams, in which he ________________ *(can, do)* better if he hadn't spent so much time on his computer. You ________________ *(need, not, tell)* him that, though – he knows it himself. After the holidays he ________________ *(must, stop)* playing video and online games for hours on end, as he ________________ *(must, start)* preparing for university, which starts in October. His younger brother Harry often asks him whether he ________________ *(may, play)* on Daniel's computer then.

66 Put into the negative.

____

____

B
You must clean the whole plate.

C
Oh no! Now we all have to change clothes!

D
I had to wait ages at the bus stop and he didn't even show up.

E
For hot meals, you have to pay in advance.

F
You must be home before ten.

Reported speech

Report-ed speech

Basics

Indirekte Rede

Die indirekte Rede wird durch bestimmte Verben eingeleitet, z. B. *add, agree, answer, continue, emphasise, go on, know, mention, point out, remark, say, state, stress, tell, think* und *want to know*. Bei der Umwandlung von direkter Rede in indirekte Rede müssen je nach Standpunkt des Sprechers / der Sprecherin auch **Pronomina, Zeitstufe** und **Adverbien** angepasst werden.

Pronouns

Die Pronomina werden folgendermaßen angepasst:

	Direct speech		Reported speech
Personalpronomen	I, you, we, you	→	he, she, they
Possessivpronomen	my, your	→	his, her
	our, your		their
Demonstrativpronomen	this	→	that
	these		those

Tenses

Ob die Zeitstufe der direkten Rede bei der Umwandlung in indirekte Rede geändert wird, hängt davon ab, in welcher Zeit das **Einleitungsverb** steht.

Keine Änderung der Zeitstufe

Steht das **Einleitungsverb** der Rede im **Präsens, Perfekt** oder **Futur**, wird die Zeitstufe der direkten Rede nicht geändert:

Tense	Direct speech		Reported speech	Tense
Present	John says / has said / will say, "I don't drive."	→	John says / has said / will say he doesn't drive.	**Present**

Änderung der Zeitstufe

Steht das **Einleitungsverb** der Rede im **Präteritum**, wird die Zeit der direkten Rede um eine Zeitstufe zurückversetzt.

Tense	Direct speech		Reported speech	Tense
Present	Ian: "I work as a designer."	→	Ian said (that) he worked as a designer.	**Simple past**
Simple past	Ian: "In 1995 I worked in advertising."	→	Ian said (that) in 1995 he had worked in advertising.	**Past perfect**
Present perfect	Ian: "I have never worked abroad."	→	Ian said (that) he had never worked abroad.	**Past perfect**
Future	Ian: "I'll visit Germany in the near future."	→	Ian said that he would visit Germany in the near future.	**Conditional**

Adverbials

Adverbiale Bestimmungen werden wie folgt angepasst:

	Direct speech		Reported speech
Adverbial phrases of time	today	→	that day
	yesterday	→	the day before
	tomorrow	→	the following day
	next week/year	→	the following week/year
	now	→	then
Adverbial of place	here	→	there

Questions

	Direct speech		Reported speech
• Fragen werden eingeleitet durch *ask, want to know, wonder.*	Ian: "How much will I earn?"	→	Ian wanted to know how much he would earn.
• Steht in der direkten Rede kein Fragepronomen, wird *if* oder *whether* eingesetzt.	Ian asked his boss: "Can I work from home?"	→	Ian asked his boss if/ whether he could work from home.

Requests, advice and commands

Aufforderungen werden durch die Konstruktion **Verb + Objekt + *(not)* Infinitiv** wiedergegeben. Das Einleitungsverb drückt aus, ob es sich um eine höfliche Aufforderung *(to ask)*, einen Rat *(to advise)* oder einen strengeren Befehl *(to tell, to order, to command)* handelt.

	Direct speech		Reported speech
• **Polite request:** Eine höfliche Aufforderung wird durch ***to ask*** eingeleitet.	She said, "Please sign the application form."	→	She asked him to sign the application form.
• **Advice:** Ein Rat wird durch ***to advise*** eingeleitet.	The doctor said, "Don't do too much overtime."	→	The doctor advised him not to do too much overtime.
• **Command:** Ein Befehl wird durch ***to order, to tell, to command*** eingeleitet.	George: "Hurry up, Jane!"	→	George told Jane to hurry up.

67 Mr Spencer, Tim's math teacher, noticed that Tim's marks were getting worse and worse. So one day he asked Tim to come and see him after the lesson. These were the teacher's questions.

a) Why are your marks getting worse?
b) Do you have any problems at home?
c) Don't you want to go to school anymore?
d) When do you go to bed at night?
e) When do you do your homework?
f) Is a parent there when you get home from school?
g) Do you see your father every day?
h) Do you have any financial worries?

In the afternoon Tim's friend Arvind asks him what Mr Spencer had wanted to know. Give Tim's answer. Start like this: "Old Spencer wanted to know / asked / inquired etc. ..."

Example:

Direct speech	**Reported speech**
What the teacher asked:	What Tim told his friend Arvind:
"How do you feel about school?"	"Old Spencer wanted to know how I felt about school."

Now you go on:

a) ____________________

b) ____________________

c) ____________________

d) ____________________

e) ____________________

f) ____________________

g) ____________________

h) ____________________

68 Tim told his teacher that he had taken a job in a supermarket to earn some extra pocket money. That was probably why he had not had enough time to do his school work properly. This is the advice Tim received from his teacher:

a) Think about what's more important: pocket money or school.

b) Tell your parents about your job!

c) Don't work too many hours!

d) Don't do any hard manual work!

e) Avoid working before you have a test at school!

f) Work on Saturdays only!

g) Avoid working late at night!

h) Don't do any shift work!

Tim tells Arvind what Old Spencer told him to do.
He told/advised me …

Example:

Direct speech	**Reported speech**
What Old Spencer advised him:	What Timothy told Arvind:
"Find an easier job!"	"He advised me to find an easier job."

Now you go on:

a) ____________________

b) ____________________

c) ____________________

d) ____________________

e) ____________________

f) ____________________

g) ____________________

h) ____________________

The gerund and the participles

Basics

Das Gerundium

Als Gerundium *(gerund)* bezeichnet man ein Verb, das zum Substantiv gemacht wurde (durch Anhängen von *-ing:* z. B. *reading* = Lesen). Das Gerundium kann als Subjekt oder Objekt verwendet werden.

The gerund as subject

Das Gerundium kann Subjekt eines Satzes sein.	Listening to music is very relaxing. *(Das) Musikhören ist sehr entspannend.*
Besonders häufig steht diese Fügung nach:	
• *there is no* = es lässt sich nicht	There is no denying that young people have more money today. *Es lässt sich nicht leugnen, dass Jugendliche heute mehr Geld haben.*
• *it's no use/no good* = es hat keinen Zweck	It's no use crying over spilt milk. *Es hat keinen Zweck, über verschüttete Milch zu weinen. (Sprichwort = Passiert ist passiert.)*
• *it's worth* = es lohnt sich	It's worth listening to their latest album. *Es lohnt sich, ihr neuestes Album anzuhören.*

The gerund after certain verbs

Es gibt eine Reihe von Verben, nach denen im Englischen das Gerundium stehen muss. Im Deutschen wird meist der Infinitiv verwendet.

admit	*zugeben*	imagine	*sich vorstellen*
anticipate	*vorwegnehmen, voraussehen*	involve	*umfassen, mit sich bringen*
avoid	*vermeiden*	keep	*fortfahren, weitermachen*
consider	*erwägen*	mind	*etw. haben gegen*
delay	*verschieben, verzögern*	miss	*vermissen*
deny	*leugnen*	postpone	*verschieben*
detest	*verabscheuen*	prevent	*(ver)hindern*
dread	*fürchten*	recollect	*sich erinnern an*
enjoy	*genießen, etw. gern tun*	resent	*übel nehmen*
excuse	*entschuldigen*	resist	*widerstehen*
fancy	*Gefallen finden an*	risk	*wagen*
feel like	*Lust haben auf*	save	*retten, bewahren*
finish	*beenden*	suggest	*vorschlagen*
forgive	*verzeihen*	understand	*verstehen*

Gerund and infinitive with different meanings

Einige Verben ändern ihre Bedeutung, je nachdem, ob Gerundium oder Infinitiv folgt.

to forget

Gerund	Infinitive
I'll never forget seeing Michael Jackson live. *Ich werde nie vergessen, wie ich einmal … sah.* *(= bezieht sich auf die Vergangenheit)*	I won't forget to buy the latest album of Adele. *Ich werde nicht vergessen (= daran denken), … zu kaufen. (= bezieht sich auf die Zukunft)*

to remember

Gerund	Infinitive
I remember seeing the film *Juno* for the first time when I was 15. *Ich erinnere mich, wie ich … gesehen habe, …*	I must remember to lend you the *Juno* DVD. *Ich muss daran denken (= darf nicht vergessen), dir … zu leihen.*

to regret

Gerund	Infinitive
I regret having missed the film on TV. *Es tut mir leid, dass ich … verpasst habe.*	I regret to miss your party next Saturday but I will be on holiday then. *Es tut mir leid, dass ich … verpassen werde.*

to stop

Gerund	Infinitive
I stopped listening to the news on the radio. *Ich hörte auf, die Nachrichten … zu hören.*	I stopped to listen to the news. *Ich hörte (mit meiner Arbeit) auf, um die Nachrichten zu hören.*

to try

Gerund	Infinitive
I won't try getting any tickets for the concert – they'll be sold out anyway. *Ich werde gar nicht probieren, Karten zu bekommen. (= einen Versuch machen)*	I've tried to get tickets for the concert – but in vain. *Ich habe (ernsthaft) versucht (= mich angestrengt), Karten zu bekommen.*

69 Decide which verb form is correct (gerund or infinitive).

Example:

Tom suggested ________ *(going/to go)* to the cinema to see the latest Bond movie.	Tom suggested going to the cinema to see the latest Bond movie.

a) Ed admitted ______________ *(having seen/to have seen)* the film before, so he didn't really feel like ______________ *(watching/to watch)* it again.

b) Tom, however, said, "I think that film is well worth ______________ *(seeing/to see)* twice."

c) But Ed wasn't convinced: "Who would want ____________ *(going/to go)* and see a film for the second time!?"

d) Anne interrupted before Tom could answer: "And what about me? Has anybody asked me what I would like ______________ *(doing/to do)* tonight?"

e) Ed: "Well, what about you then? Would you prefer ______________ *(going/to go)* to the cinema, to a disco or to a restaurant?"

f) Anne: "I don't fancy ______________ *(sitting/to sit)* in a dark cinema for three hours. And I can't imagine the two of you ______________ *(dancing/to dance)* with me in the 'The Millenium Club'! So let's go to MacBeef's!"

g) Tom: "I detest ____________________ *(eating/to eat)* fast food that tastes of nothing!"

h) Ed: "If you don't enjoy ____________________ *(eating/to eat)* out, why don't you stay at home!"

i) Finally Anne said, "Oh, stop ________________ *(arguing/to argue)*. Let's go and see the film, have a snack and go to the disco afterwards."

70 Replace the underlined words with the expressions given in brackets. Supply the right preposition if necessary and use the gerund.

Example:

It's impossible to know in advance if a song will hit the charts. *(There's no way)*	There's no way of knowing in advance if a song will hit the charts.

a) I think many young people would like to play in a pop group. *(to enjoy)*

____

b) One day my friends Jeff and Morris suggested forming a pop group because we like to make music. *(to be interested)*

____

c) They thought it would not be too difficult for us to play a couple of numbers together. *(to have no difficulty)*

____

d) We didn't really know what songs to choose, but one night Jeff suggested, "Couldn't we pick some golden oldies that everybody likes?" *(How about)*

____

e) In the end, we managed to rehearse some old Stones numbers. *(to succeed)*

____

f) We are excited we're going to play at our youth club next Friday. *(to look forward)*

____

Basics

Das Partizip Präsens und Partizip Perfekt

Partizipien werden häufig benutzt, um Relativsätze und Adverbialsätze zu verkürzen.

Zwischen zwei Formen muss unterschieden werden:

- **Partizip Präsens** (= Infinitiv + *ing*, z. B. *driving, offering, singing)*
- **Partizip Perfekt** (= Infinitiv + *-ed, -d* bzw. bei unregelmäßigen Verben 3. Form der Stammformen, z. B. *driven, offered, sung)*

Relative clauses

Aktivsätze werden mit dem **Partizip Präsens** verkürzt.

long version	shortened version
David Livingstone was the man who opened up the African Continent.	David Livingstone was the man opening up the African Continent.

David Livingstone war der Mann, der den afrikanischen Kontinent erschloss.

Passivsätze werden mit dem **Partizip Perfekt** verkürzt.

long version	shortened version
Livingstone criticised the slave trade which was carried on by some traders.	Livingstone criticised the slave trade carried on by some traders.

Livingston kritisierte den Sklavenhandel, der von einigen Händlern weiterhin betrieben wurde.

Adverbial clauses

Adverbiale Nebensätze können mit einer Partizipialkonstruktion verkürzt werden.

Adverbialsatz der Zeit

Wenn man einen temporalen Adverbialsatz verkürzt, muss man besonders auf das Zeitverhältnis (*time relation*) achten, in dem die Handlung des Nebensatzes zur Handlung des Hauptsatzes steht.

Das **Partizip Präsens** drückt aus, dass zwei Handlungen **gleichzeitig** verlaufen.

long version	shortened version
As the explorers shared their last water supplies, they talked about crossing the desert more quickly.	Sharing their last water supplies, the explorers talked about crossing the desert more quickly. or: When sharing their last water supplies, …

Als die Forscher ihre letzten Wasservorräte teilten, sprachen sie darüber, wie sie die Wüste schneller durchqueren könnten.

***Having* + Partizip Perfekt** drückt aus, dass eine Handlung **zeitlich vor** einer zweiten liegt (d. h. sie war bereits abgeschlossen, als die andere begann).

long version	shortened version
After the explorers had used up their water supplies, they talked about crossing the desert more quickly.	Having used up their water supplies, the explorers talked about crossing the desert more quickly. or: After using up their water supplies, …

Nachdem die Forscher ihre Wasservorräte aufgebraucht hatten, fragten sie sich, wie sie die Wüste schneller durchqueren könnten.

Beachte: In der deutschen Übersetzung steht üblicherweise im Nebensatz das Substantiv, im Hauptsatz das Pronomen.

Having used up all their water supplies, the explorers wanted to get to the missionary station as quickly as possible.
Nachdem die Forscher ihre gesamten Wasservorräte aufgebraucht hatten, wollten sie so schnell wie möglich die Missionsstation erreichen.

Adverbialsatz des Grundes

Um den Grund einer Handlung in verkürzter Form auszudrücken, kann man ebenfalls eine **Partizipialkonstruktion** verwenden.

long version	shortened version
As Livingstone felt exhausted, he told his servants to build a hut.	Feeling exhausted, Livingstone told his servants to build a hut.

Da Livingstone erschöpft war, wies er seine Diener an, eine Hütte zu bauen.

71 Shorten these sentences. Replace the relative and adverbial clauses by a different construction.

Example:

Tourists who travel to Africa want to watch wild animals in their natural surroundings.	Tourists **travelling** to Africa want to watch wild animals in their natural surroundings.

a) An international convention which was held in New York banned the sale of ivory.

b) Tourists who are interested in watching herds of elephants were pleased about the news.

c) As many African countries depend on tourism, they profited from the ban.

d) International organisations like Greenpeace which supported the move in general also pointed out some problems which arose from the ban.

e) As the countries increased the number of protected regions, they attracted more tourists.

f) The arrival of larger numbers of tourists spoiled parts of the areas that were meant to be protected.

72 Replace the underlined participle constructions by using relative or adverbial clauses.

Example:

The war against poaching <u>begun</u> by US naturalists many years ago has not been won in all states.	The war against poaching **which was begun** by US naturalists many years ago has not been won in all states.

a) The campaign for the protection of apes and rhinos <u>started</u> by US and Japanese scientists attracted the interest of the world public.

____

____

b) Cameramen made TV films <u>showing</u> the cruelties of poachers in the national parks.

____

____

c) Having seen the pictures, TV viewers wrote letters of protest.

d) The civil war taking place in Rwanda almost destroyed one of the last habitats of African mountain gorillas.

e) Not having enough land to grow food, farmers invaded Rwanda's Volcanoes National Park.

f) The rebels seizing control of the park were Tutsis, an ethnic group trying to get back land lost more than three decades ago.

g) They destroyed a research centre run for nearly two decades by the American naturalist Dian Fossey, whose pioneering work with the great apes was made famous by the film *Gorillas in the Mist*.

Language in Use: Vocabulary

Test your vocabulary knowledge

73 Cloze-Test: Working for social reforms

Complete the text with words from the list.

> aware • experienced • search • educated • century • increased • misery • underprivileged • debts • injustices • prison • wages • dreadful • introduce

The 19th ______________ – the Victorian Age – was a time of great prosperity in England. The population ______________ tremendously: in 1811 England had 12 million inhabitants, by 1851 that number had risen to 21 million. The Industrial Revolution and the growth of the Empire made factory owners and merchants rich. Under the golden surface there was a lower class whose life was characterised by poverty, ______________ and crime. Thousands of workers left the countryside in ______________ of jobs in the towns. What they found were low ______________ and badly built houses. The little money they earned was not enough to support themselves and their families. If they could not pay their ______________, they had to go to ______________. Gradually, more and more ______________ people became aware of the great ______________ and the social problems of the age and tried to ______________ reforms. An important member of that reform movement was one of the greatest writers of English literature: Charles Dickens. In his very popular novels Dickens described the ______________ conditions in which poor people had to live. He wanted to make his readers ______________ that social reforms were necessary to improve the lives of the ______________ masses. Dickens knew very well what he was writing about because in his early childhood he had ______________ what it meant to be poor.

74 C-Test: The real Robinson Crusoe

In the following text, a lot of words are incomplete. Try to restore them relying on both your language skills and the context given. Half the letters of the incomplete words are already given.

Alexander Selkirk was the son of a shoemaker born in Largo in the Fife region in Scotland. As a young boy, he was hard to control and got into trouble with almost everyone. After arg_____ with ma_____ of h_____ neighbours, h_____ left ho_____ and r_____ away t_____ sea. Selkirk w_____ 19 ye_____ of a_____ then.
In 1703, he bec_____ a sai_____ on a pir_____ ship, but co_____ not st_____ the disci_____ on bo_____. After a_____ argument wi_____ the cap_____, he ask_____ to b_____ put ash_____ on t_____ nearest isl_____. He wan_____ to li_____ on h_____ own. The sh_____ was ne_____ the Juan Fernández Isl_____, off t_____ coast o_____ Chile. In Oct_____ 1704, Selkirk w_____ left beh_____ on an uninh_____ island, a beau_____ place wi_____ rich veget_____. There we_____ plenty o_____ goats wh_____ Selkirk co_____ hunt. There we_____ no peo_____ at a_____ and Selkirk enj_____ the sil_____. After mo_____ than 4 ye_____ of be_____ alone, h_____ decided th_____ he h_____ had eno_____. In 1709, he s_____ two sh_____ off t_____ coast and l_____ a fi_____ to att_____ their atte_____. One o_____ the sh_____ sent a bo_____ ashore t_____ pick u_____ Alexander Selkirk. It to_____ him ba_____ to civili_____ again. He di_____ in 1721.
The Eng_____ writer Daniel Defoe he_____ of Selkirk's st_____ and wr_____ a no_____ based o_____ Selkirk's exper_____. He called it *The Life and Strange Surprising Adventures of Robinson Crusoe*.

75 Anagram: Discovery

The letters of these words have been jumbled. Write down the original words using the definitions to help you.

Anagram	Word	Definition
A ACHERS		to look through or go over thoroughly to find sth
B CYOVNO		a group of ships or lorries travelling together or under protection
C EPEDXINOIT		a journey undertaken for the purpose of research
D GEUERF		a safe place from danger or trouble
E PAOLRPSO		an offer, a suggestion
F YLPUPS		a store of things needed
G TCARE		a track or a mark left by sth or sb
H ISDOVREC		to find sth new

76 Cloze-Test: Tintagel today

Complete the text with words from this list.

board • enemies • path • view • born • fascinated • remains • waves • coast • location • situated • connection • meetings • stone

For centuries the impressive ______________ of the castle has ______________ visitors from all over the country. It is ______________ high on a hill on the rough ______________ of Cornwall near the little village of Tintagel: People call it "King Arthur's castle". However, when you have climbed the steep ______________ to the top there is not much to see today: a number of low ______________ walls which might be the ______________ of a hall, of a well and perhaps a few graves. What is more breathtaking is the fantastic ______________ of the rocks and the sea – and the thought of a legendary ______________ between the castle and King Arthur. Could this be the place where Arthur was ______________, where Merlin, the magician, hid the baby from his ______________? "Merlin's Cave" is the name of a rock formation down by the ____________ that you can see from the top of the castle. Is this the place where King Arthur and his Knights of the Round Table held their ____________? At least this is what the villagers of Tintagel and the local tourist ____________ would have you believe.

C-Test: From now on some words are incomplete. Only one or a few of letters are given. Try to complete the text with words that fit the context.

It all be____________ in the 12th century, when Geoffrey of Monmouth reco____________ the legend of King Arthur in his *History of the Kings of Britain*. He made Tintagel the scene where it all happ________. Many writers foll______ who took up the story of Arthur and his great court at Camelot, among them Alfred Lord Tennyson (1809–1892). Bet________ 1859 and 1888 he completed *Idylls of the King*, an Arthurian epic in 12 pa________. All romantic writers of the nineteenth century kept al________ the traditional conne________ with Tintagel Castle, not knowing what had rea______ happened in the past. There was no scien________ proof, as archae__________ was still in its infancy. However, the stories became extremely pop________, and the link between Arthur and Tintagel was stro________ than ever.

Scrambled Letters: Restore the original word. The first letter is already given.

Archaeologists began *(e-ianaxsovct)* ______________ at Tintagel in 1933. They found out that the *(r-nuis)* __________ we see today are the remains of a Norman *(c-taels)* ____________ built in the 12th century. The *(q-suinote)* ______________, though, is why did Reginald, Earl of Cornwall, build a castle at a *(p-clea)* _________ which is of little strategic *(v-auel)* _________? Moreover, the castle could not have been an *(i-nmotrpat)* ______________ one because it was only used for a relatively *(s-rhto)* ____________ time. People lived in it for only a *(h-edudrn)* ____________ years or so and by the fourteenth century it had *(f-lanel)* ____________ into disrepair. Later it was used as a *(p-snroi)* ____________. So, that medieval castle could not have been Arthur's castle after all! If Arthur were not just a legendary *(f-ugier)*

__________, he would have lived in the sixth century, well before Tintagel was *(b-ltui)* __________. Consequently, the *(l-kin)* __________ that Geoffrey had made was the result of *(c-moeeplt)* __________ fantasy.

77 Word field: The world of work

Complete these words and find them in the word square.

ME___L	H__E	IL________
AB__E	EM___Y	DI______D
IN___Y	PE___T	RE________N
E__N	CO_____N	UN______D
L___UR	FA____Y	EX__________
FI___Y	PO____Y	

U

R E N

A E E A S

C B X M S R K

F O U P P G T N I

I I M S L L D T R E L

D N L P E O O I K T I Y L

J Q J T L F I Y S A P H C Y E

R R M U H A S T T R I O A P T Y D

X P O P R Y I T A E E F S P R K I G C

N E O B Z Y V N Z T N G S O C W Y V O C J

F A C T O R Y I I A A P O V E R T Y N

M G P F C L O O U R A P L E U P K

Z M Z L P M N X D D T F V R N

K I I O G B M D R L Y U P

C G H K M E P A N O T

H I L A N K X B I

I T O I M A M

R K A L R

E L E

P

78 Anagrams

The letters of these words have been jumbled. Write down the original words using the definitions to help you.

Anagram	Word	Definition
A BUERHPSLI		a person or a company that produces and distributes copies of a book, newspaper, etc. for sale
B AHGETR		to come together; to collect sth; to pick sth (e.g. flowers)
C RUSOEC		a spring or fountainhead from which a stream issues
D GURTOHD		a long time without any rain; dry weather
E AEBCMRE		to hold sb close, esp. as a sign of affection
F MEUSEPR		to suppose that sth is true; to take sth for granted
G MIAATSN		physical or moral strength to resist or withstand illness, fatigue, or hardship; endurance
H UGNEJL		tropical forest that is very dense and hard to get through
I PUTOPIOLAN		the total number of inhabitants in a country or individuals living in an area

79 Crossword puzzle

Solve the crossword puzzle.

Across:
1 sammeln
3 fliehen, entkommen; Flucht
7 Bevölkerung
9 beten
12 Interesse
16 errichten, einrichten
17 Missionar
19 verlegen sein
22 entfernt
24 Vieh, Rinder
25 Wunsch, Anfrage
29 leiden
30 Abschaffung
31 Verteidiger
32 Forscher

Down:
2 retten
4 Pionier
5 Dürre
6 (Land-)Karte
8 vermuten, annehmen
10 Verleger
11 Wildnis
13 schließlich
14 Ausdauer
15 Dschungel
18 inner(e, er, es); Landesinnere
20 sich erholen
21 sich umarmen
23 Grausamkeit
26 ereignisreich
27 Quelle, Ursprung
28 nachladen, neu laden

How to paraphrase

Basics

Informationen in eigenen Worten ausdrücken

How to find synonyms and write paraphrases

Die Aufgabenstellungen in diesem Bereich testen Ihren Wortschatz. Sie sollen bestimmte Wörter durch ähnliche *(synonyms)* ersetzen bzw. in anderen Worten denselben Inhalt ausdrücken *(paraphrase)*. Diese Techniken können Sie sowohl in schriftlichen als auch mündlichen Prüfungen gut gebrauchen, z. B. wenn Sie den Inhalt eines Textes in eigenen Worten zusammenfassen sollen oder wenn Sie sich Ihrem Vorredner anschließen wollen, ohne seine Ausführungen komplett zu wiederholen.

Synonyms

- Finden Sie ein „sinnverwandtes" Wort, das in dem gegebenen Zusammenhang dieselbe Bedeutung hat.
- Wenn Sie innerhalb eines Satzes ein Wort ersetzen sollen, dann achten Sie genau auf den umgebenden Text. Achten Sie auch auf Zeitformen, Singular- bzw. Pluralformen.
- Wenn Ihnen die Bedeutung des Wortes, für das Sie ein Synonym angeben sollen, nicht geläufig ist, nutzen Sie die Information, die der Kontext bietet. Überlegen Sie sich, was das Wort wahrscheinlich bedeutet.

The Queen delivered a speech.
The Queen made/gave a speech.

Paraphrase

- Eine Paraphrase ist eine erklärende Umschreibung, mit der Sie einen Begriff *(word)*, eine Wendung *(phrase)* oder auch den Inhalt eines Textabschnitts *(passage)* verdeutlichen sollen. Anders als bei *synonyms* brauchen Sie sich nicht an die Wortstellung des Ausgangstextes zu halten, sondern können freier formulieren und umstellen.

The European Union and the United States have increased foreign aid programmes. = The European Union and the United States have given more development aid.

I am sorry I could not do my homework in time as I was ill yesterday. =
The pupil claimed that doing his/her homework had been impossible due to illness.

80 Synonyms and definitions: Child crime

Criminologists say that in the majority of cases violent crimes are committed by youngsters who come from a poor background. Even more important than the depressing economic situation is the sad fact that most young delinquents come from broken homes. They grow up without love. Nobody tells them what is right and what is wrong. They have the feeling that nobody is really interested in them, no-one cares. When they play truant and don't turn up at school – nobody seems to mind or exercise some sort of control.

Another explanation for child crime is that young people learn violent behaviour. By watching violence in films or videos which are meant for "adults only", children get used to brutality and find it entertaining. Very often parents do not care what sort of films or videos their children watch.

Some teachers argue that computer games have a negative influence on young children. Those computer games which offer brutality are popular and can be bought quite easily. Children can become aggressive by constantly playing such computer games.

a) Find and highlight synonyms for:
- youngsters (l. 2)
- delinquents (l. 3)
- entertaining (l. 10)
- depressing (l. 3)
- homes (l. 4)

b) Explain what these words mean:
- criminologist (l. 1)
- to play truant (l. 6)

81 Multiple matching

Find a paraphrase that fits one of the words in the left-hand column.

Word	Order	Paraphrase
stupid		1 to say one will do harm if a person does not do what is desired
divorce		2 opposite of intelligent, clever
gossip		3 the good and evil that happens to people; great wealth
deprive		4 legal separation of husband and wife by court of law
threaten		5 useless talk, usually about other people and their mistakes
fortune		6 causing anger; insulting and disgusting
offensive		7 to take away from sb

Word formation: prefixes and suffixes

Basics

Wortbildung mittels Vor- und Nachsilben

Durch Voranstellen von Präfixen oder Anhängen von Suffixen kann man das Gegenteil eines Wortes oder eine andere Wortart bilden. Prä- und Suffixe sind Elemente, die nicht alleine stehen können (*-ment, -able* etc.). Wenn Sie sich solche Wortbildungselemente und deren Kombinationsmöglichkeiten einprägen, vergrößert sich schnell Ihr Wortschatz.

Word formation with prefixes

Die wichtigsten Vorsilben sind ***un-***, ***mis-***, ***dis-*** und ***in-***. Die Vorsilbe ***in-*** stellt eine Besonderheit dar: Vor *b, p* und *m* wird *in-* zu *im-* (*impossible*), vor *l* zu *il-* (*illiterate*) und vor *r* zu *ir-* (*irrelevant*). Es gibt keine allgemein gültige Regel, welches Präfix verwendet wird.

Word formation with prefixes expressing the opposite

	nouns	verbs	adjectives
un-	unemployment	untie	unfair
in-	independence	invalidate	inedible
im-	impossibility	immobilise	impolite
il-	illiteracy	---	illogical
ir-	irregularity	---	irresponsible
mis-	misfortune	misbehave	mistaken
dis-	dislike	disobey	dishonest

Word formation with suffixes

Um ein Wort in eine andere Wortart umzuwandeln, wird ein bestimmtes Suffix angehängt. Dabei kann es zu Änderungen in der Schreibung kommen (z. B. *to enter → entrance*).

Word formation with suffixes: Nouns

-ance/-ence	-ation	-dom	-hood	-ment
distance	operation	wisdom	childhood	treatment
difference	representation	freedom	neighbourhood	fulfilment

-ness	-ty
blindness	honesty
darkness	cruelty

Word formation with suffixes: Adjectives

-ly	-ic(al)	-ous	-ful	-able/-ible
lovely	historic(al)	dangerous	careful	drinkable
yearly	economic(al)	glorious	beautiful	responsible

-al/-ial	-y	-ive
educational	cloudy	attractive
essential	hairy	constructive

82 Add a prefix to these nouns to give them the opposite meaning.

advantage		decision	
ability		honour	
appearance		literacy	
balance		patience	

83 Add a prefix to these verbs to give them the opposite meaning.

agree		do	
appear		like	
believe		plug	
connect		understand	

84 Add a prefix to these adjectives to give them the opposite meaning.

convenient		educated	
able		happy	
breakable		legal	
dependent		pleasant	

85 Add a suffix to these words to form nouns.

certain		free	
employ		pay	
enter		real	
foolish		sick	

86 Add a suffix to these nouns or verbs to form adjectives.

act		forget	
centre		noise	
comic		poison	
courage		read	

Combinations and collocations

Basics

Sprachverwendung im Kontext

Usage of words

Für ein deutsches Wort gibt es im Englischen zuweilen mehrere Entsprechungen. Welche Variante die richtige ist, ergibt sich aus dem jeweiligen Sinnzusammenhang.

bringen = *to bring, to take*

Das deutsche Wort **bringen** kann im Englischen entweder durch ***to bring*** oder durch ***to take*** wiedergegeben werden.

- Man verwendet *to bring*, wenn etwas **zum / zur Sprechenden** gebracht werden soll,

  Could you bring me that book, please?
  Könntest du mir bitte dieses Buch bringen?

- *to take*, wenn etwas **vom / von der Sprechenden weg**gebracht werden soll.

  Please take this parcel to the post office.
  Bitte bringe dieses Päckchen zur Post.

Combinations and collocations

Phrases with "to take"

to take place	*stattfinden*
to take advantage of sth	*etw. ausnutzen*
to take sth up	*etw. anfangen*
to take sth for granted	*etw. als selbstverständlich hinnehmen*
to take sth into account	*etw. berücksichtigen*
to take interest in sth	*sich interessieren für etw.*
to take care of sb	*für jdn. sorgen*
to take time (for sth)	*Zeit verwenden für etw., dauern*

87 Make up your mind: "To take" or "to bring"?

Use a form of "to take" or "to bring" in these sentences.

a) The film *Mutiny on the Bounty* ______________ fame to the actors Charles Laughton and Clark Gable.

b) We are having a party on Saturday. Please come and ______________ your girlfriend Eve, too.

c) I'm sorry about your headache. Let's finish our meal and then I'll ________ you home.

d) Robbie, please ________________ me the coat you wore at the playground. Let me check if it has to be ________________ to the cleaner's.

e) As it was getting rather late, my father ______________ Anne and Robert to the station in his car.

f) John visited me in hospital and ______________ me some lovely flowers.

g) Our history teacher is ______________ us on a trip to Rome next month.

88 Collocations with "to take": Multiple matching

Match the collocation to an expression that has the same meaning.

A to take place	1 to make good use of a favourable circumstance; to exploit or outwit sb, esp. unfairly
B to take advantage of sth	2 to believe that sth is true or valid
C to take up sth	3 to consider sth
D to take sth for granted	4 to look after; to keep safe
E to take sth into account	5 to occur, to happen
F to take care of sth	6 to require or to use up, to last
G to take time	7 to start sth, to begin sth

A	B	C	D	E	F	G

89 Make up your mind: a lot of/lots of/plenty of – much – many

Use the proper expression in these sentences.

John Red Cloud Walcott is a Native American activist. He works towards improving the situation of Native Americans in the reservations. In 1992, in his speech to commemorate the 500th anniversary of the landing of Columbus on American soil, he said:

"Even the US President admits that there is too ______________ poverty among the Native Americans. But why doesn't anyone do anything? We all know what happened in the past. There have been ______________ TV reports about the cruel treatment of American Indians by the pioneers. ______________ people know that the arrival of the Europeans did not do the Indians ______________ good! For so ______________ years they have been neglected. How ______________ longer do they have to wait for better opportunities? Why don't they receive as ______________ support as other ethnic minorities? Is it because there aren't too ________________ of us left to have political influence? Most politicians do ________________ talking but don't offer ________________ help. There aren't ________________ Native American families who live comfortable and wealthy lives. Native Americans have ________________ trouble when they try to find a job. How ________________ employers prefer a coloured applicant to a white jobseeker?"

90 Cloze-Test: Phrases with "have"

Use a phrase by combining "have" with an expression from the box.

a cold • a drink • fun • a holiday • a rest • a talk • it done

a) I'm terribly thirsty – I must ________________ right away!

b) Dad isn't pleased with your coming home so late every night. He wants to ________________ to you.

c) Shirley, you have worked very hard these last few hours; ________________!

d) We don't have to do all this work ourselves, boss. I'll ________________ for us.

e) My nose keeps running; I think I ________________.

f) Anne and Robert have been married for eight years and they have never gone abroad in the summer. But this year they'll ________________ in France.

g) You went to the disco last night, didn't you? Did you ________________?

91 German "machen"

Which verbs go with which nouns? Write the nouns in the proper places.

a photo(graph) • an exam • a mistake • a course • an offer • a film • a break • one's best • one's (home)work • a noise • an effort • one's hair • notes • the best of sth

do	make	take

92 Cloze-Test: Phrases with "to do"

Use a phrase by combining a form of "do" with an expression from the box.

the dishes • one's hair • one's homework • for a living • the shopping • well

a) The fridge is almost empty! Before we start cooking, we need to ______________ first.

b) My sister spends three hours in front of the mirror to ______________.

c) That was a tasty meal, Jim. But now I feel really tired. Could you help me ______________, please?

d) You've worked so hard. I hope you ______________ in your exam.

e) The Taylors seem to have loads of money. Do you happen to know what Mr. Taylor ______________?

f) Greg, before you leave for school: Have you ______________ for today?

False friends

Basics

Falsche Entsprechungen in Mutter- und Fremdsprache

sea – lake

- *sea* = das Meer, die See
  Sea wird verwendet zur Bezeichnung eines salzigen Gewässers, z. B. *the North Sea, the Dead Sea*. Nur selten wird ein Binnensee *sea* genannt: *the Sea of Galilee*.

Unfortunately, we cannot cross the Channel tunnel by boat today as the sea is too rough.
Leider können wir den Ärmelkanal heute nicht mit dem Schiff überqueren, da das Meer zu hohen Wellengang hat.

- *lake* = der See
  Der See, also das Gewässer, das von Land umgeben ist, wird als *lake* bezeichnet, z. B. *Lake Constance* (Bodensee), *Lake Geneva* (Genfer See), *Lake District in Cumbria*.

They went down to the lake.
Sie stiegen hinab zum See.

happy – lucky

- *happy* = glücklich
  Happy wird verwendet zur Bezeichnung eines Gefühlszustands.

Arthur was very happy when they told him that he was the new king.
Artus war sehr glücklich (froh), als man ihm sagte, er sei der neue König.

- *lucky* = glücklich
  Lucky bedeutet Glück haben, auf das man selbst keinen Einfluss hat.

It was lucky he won the lottery.
Er hatte das Glück, im Lotto zu gewinnen.

hear – listen

- *hear* = hören
  Hear bezeichnet die Fähigkeit des Hörens.

Can you hear me at the back?
Können Sie mich da hinten hören?

- *listen* = zuhören
  Listen bezeichnet das bewusste Zuhören, z. B. bei einem Vortrag.

Please listen to what I'm saying!
Hör mal bitte zu, was ich sage!

93 Choose the right words to fill the gaps.

a) Thousands of poor Cuban migrants try to sail across the ____________ *(lake/sea)* to America.

b) The Everglades once covered the entire tip of Florida – about 4 million acres of wetland stretching from ______________ *(Lake/Sea)* Okeechobee in the north to the Gulf of Mexico in the south.

c) Lois cries, "Superman, if you can _____________ *(hear/listen to)* me, drop what you're doing and help me!"

d) British generals proposed a military land, ______________ *(lake/sea)* and air blockade to fight the dictatorial regime.

e) Our teacher never has time to ______________ *(hear/listen to)* the worries and concerns of his students.

f) Scientists suspect that pesticides and other toxic chemicals are discharged into rivers and out to _____________ *(lake/sea)*, killing marine life.

g) Lots of immigrants would be _____________ *(happy/ lucky)* to work for money or food.

h) Billy Graham would practise sermons aloud in old sheds or in a canoe in the middle of a _____________ *(lake/sea)*.

i) Nelson Mandela only used violence when the other side would not _____________ *(hear/listen)*.

j) After the shooting, the criminal threw the gun into a __________ *(lake/sea)*.

k) Did you _____________ *(hear/listen)* the story of the tourist who got lost in the maze at Hampton Court?

94 The curse of the dead pharaoh

Choose the right word to fill in the gaps. Put the verbs into the right tense.

(to) become – (to) obtain • actually – current • eventually – perhaps

The early death of Lord Carnarvon, sponsor of Howard Carter, __________ the starting point of a legend: that of "the curse of the pharaoh". Shortly after its discovery in 1922, the tomb of the pharaoh had ______________ the status of a world sensation. Millions of readers wanted to know everything about the ______________ state of the excavations. Thousands of visitors ______________ travelled to Egypt to have a look at the site themselves. ____________________ a journalist got so bored with ordinary reports on the diggings that when yet another member of Carter's crew – Archibald Reid – died, he invented a sensational headline: "Has Reid ___________ another victim of the curse of Tutankhamen?" A new "mystery" was created:

Everyone who had taken part in the opening of the tomb would not ______________ old. The ghost of the dead pharaoh would ______________ cause his early death. That was the punishment for those who had ______________ access to the burial chamber. In the 1930s the general public had ______________ so interested in the mysterious deaths that Hollywood producers ________________ made films on the subject. The film *The Mummy* (1932), for example, was to _______________ a horror classic. Today we know that all 20 people in Carter's crew ________________ died natural deaths: due to infections, illnesses or even suicide. The mysterious deaths have thus been explained, but the Valley of Kings has ________________ more secrets in store.

95 The tragedy of Marilyn Monroe

Use the right word to fill in the empty spaces.

Few people would say that Marilyn Monroe's acting was ______________ *(famous/ excellent)*, but according to the ____________ *(meaning/opinion)* of actors who played in films alongside her, she was a ______________ *(sensible/ sensitive)* creature. It is true, though, that she was hard to work with. Most of all, her extravagance was due to the cruel treatment she had received from ______________ *(scrupulous/unscrupulous)* photographers and managers since she first started as a starlet and pin-up girl.

She was born on June 1, 1926 as Norma Jean Baker, an illegitimate child who never knew her father. Growing up in poverty and misery didn't help her to develop any ________________ *(self-confidence/self-consciousness)*.

A 21-year-old aircraft plant worker ________________ *(became/got)* her hero and rescued her from that dreadful background. Norma Jean married him when she was 16 and began working as a model for bathing costumes.

In order to ________________ *(become/get)* famous and earn more money she also started posing for pin-ups and glamour photos. A Hollywood producer saw her photos, offered her a contract and renamed her Marilyn Monroe.

At first she was only given smaller roles because of the stiff ________________ *(concurrence/competition)* in the film industry, but eventually she played in major films, usually taking the role of the dumb blonde. Millions liked to see her that way and queued in front of the cinemas to buy ________________ *(cards/tickets)* for her latest film.

On August 5, 1962, she committed suicide by taking an overdose of sleeping pills, worried about getting old and losing her sex appeal. She had always relied on other people's ______________ *(meaning/opinion)* too much. She had never found her own role in life, had always acted a part.

Linkers

Basics

Verknüpfungen zwischen zwei Sätzen

Ein Text besteht nicht einfach aus einer gewissen Anzahl von beliebig aneinander gereihten Sätzen. Vielmehr stellt er ein enges Geflecht von aufeinander bezogenen Einzelteilen dar. Logische Verweise halten die Sätze zusammen. Mithilfe dieser Satzverknüpfungen können die Leser*innen den Ausführungen des Autors / der Autorin besser folgen.

Bei der Textproduktion muss deutlich werden, dass die Einzelsätze in einer logischen Beziehung zueinander stehen, dass sie miteinander verbunden sind. Erst durch eine angemessene und richtige Verwendung sogenannter **linkage words** (*to link* = verbinden) wird aus Einzelsätzen ein zusammenhängender Text.

Ein kurzer Beispieltext soll Ihnen zeigen, wie die einzelnen Sätze eines Abschnitts miteinander verbunden sein können:

Columbus believed he had reached the East Indies. Consequently, he called the inhabitants of the islands "Indians". For a long time, this term was in general use when people referred to the indigenous peoples of North, Central and South America. We call them "Native Americans" now.

Eine Analyse der Satzfunktionen macht das Beziehungsgeflecht und die Verweise klar:

Satz		Analyse
1	Columbus believed he had reached the East Indies.	
2	**Consequently, he** called the inhabitants of the islands "Indians".	*eine doppelte Verbindung zum vorherigen Satz:* ***Consequently*** *= Folge aus erstem Satz;* ***he*** *= Bezug auf die im ersten Satz genannte Person „Columbus"*
3	For a long time, **this** term was in general use when people referred to the indigenous peoples of North, Central and South America.	*bezieht sich auf „Indians" im zweiten Satz*
4	We call **them** "Native Americans".	*verweist auf „indigenous peoples" im dritten Satz*

Im Folgenden werden Ihnen einige Möglichkeiten aufgezeigt, wie Sie Sätze – je nach Aussageabsicht – verbinden können.

Aussageabsicht	Linkage words
einen **Gedanken** hinzufügen	also *(nicht am Satzanfang)*, besides, further, furthermore, in addition, in the same way, moreover
einen **Gedanken** neu formulieren	in other words, that means, that is, that is to say
einen **Gedankengang** abschließen	in brief, in conclusion, in short, on the whole
die **Reihenfolge** verdeutlichen	first, second, etc.; next, finally, in the end

das **Gegenteil** ausdrücken	however, in contrast, in spite of, on the contrary, on the other hand, yet
einen **Vergleich** anstellen	in the same way, likewise, similarly
eine **Folgerung** ausdrücken	as a result, consequently, hence, therefore
eine **Einräumung** ausdrücken	after all, although, even if, in any case, though
eine **Bedingung** ausdrücken	if, in case that, provided that, unless
eine zeitliche **Verbindung** knüpfen	after, as soon as, at last, before, eventually, in the end, in the past, lately, recently, when, while
eine **Begründung** anführen	because, for this reason, since, that is why, therefore
ein **Beispiel** anführen	for example, for instance, in other words

96 Linking sentences: American Indians today

Choose the linkage word that you think fits best.

What the Spaniards and the other conquerors did to the native population and their culture has not been forgotten. The 500th anniversary of the explorers' first landing on American shores (1992) had been planned as a great celebration. *(However – Therefore – Besides)* ______________, Columbus Day, October 12, became a day of protest. Native Americans and other groups staged big demonstrations *(although – because – unless)* ____________ they wanted to remind the world of the genocide of their people. *(That means – On the whole – Secondly)* ______________ they see the arrival of Columbus and his successors as the tragic beginning of the extinction of many indigenous peoples of America.

To the soldiers and settlers of the westward movement the Indians were wild, stupid creatures. *(However – Since – Hence)* ______________, words like those of Indian Chief Seattle prove that the Indians really knew better: "We know that the white man does not understand our ways. One portion of land is the same to him as the next, *(for – however – while)* ______________ he is a stranger who comes in the night and takes from the land whatever he needs. The earth is not his brother, *(though – besides – but)* ______________ his enemy, and *(when – provided that – although)* ______________________ he has conquered it, he moves on."

Today, the two million American Indians form one of the smallest ethnic groups in the United States. *(As a result – In contrast – In addition)* ______________ they have hardly any influence on modern American society. *(Though – Unless – For instance)* ________________ all of us support the just cause of the Native Americans, their life in the reservations will still be characterised by extreme poverty, mass unemployment, alcoholism and suicide.

97 Structuring a text: Killing off the native population

Connect the sentences by choosing suitable connectors from the box – you might also change their structure.

furthermore • to begin with • however • in addition • moreover • for example • as a result (of) • therefore • despite • whereas • apart from • because (of)

a) At the end of the 15th century, there were still about 100 million Native Americans.

b) The Mayas and Aztecs lived in the territory that is now Mexico, the Incas had settled in western South America, including modern Peru and parts of Ecuador, Chile and Argentina.

c) The arrival of European settlers changed the life of the Native Americans for the worse. Their number declined dramatically.

d) Just two hundred years after Columbus set foot on the Bahamas there were only four million natives left.

e) The Native Americans were robbed of their land by the European settlers, who drove native people away into the less fertile areas.

f) Many died of infectious diseases, such as measles, brought by the Europeans.

g) Others did not survive the cruel treatment they suffered as slaves or were killed by the settlers who used firearms against them in battles.

Writing

An email about what really matters to young Australians

98 Every year the community service organisation Mission Australia asks Australian teenagers between the ages of 15 and 19 about matters that play an important role in their lives. Your Australian e-pal participated in the survey and has sent you the following screenshots of the published results, asking whether you share the attitudes described below.

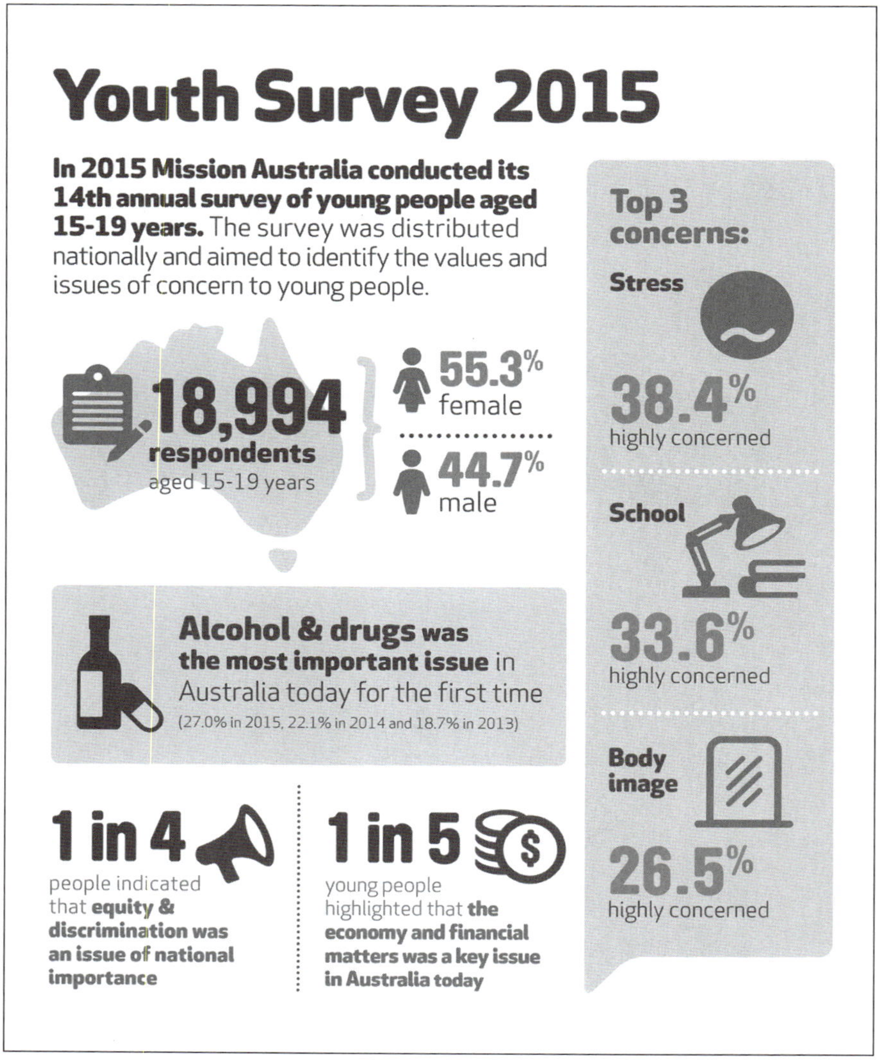

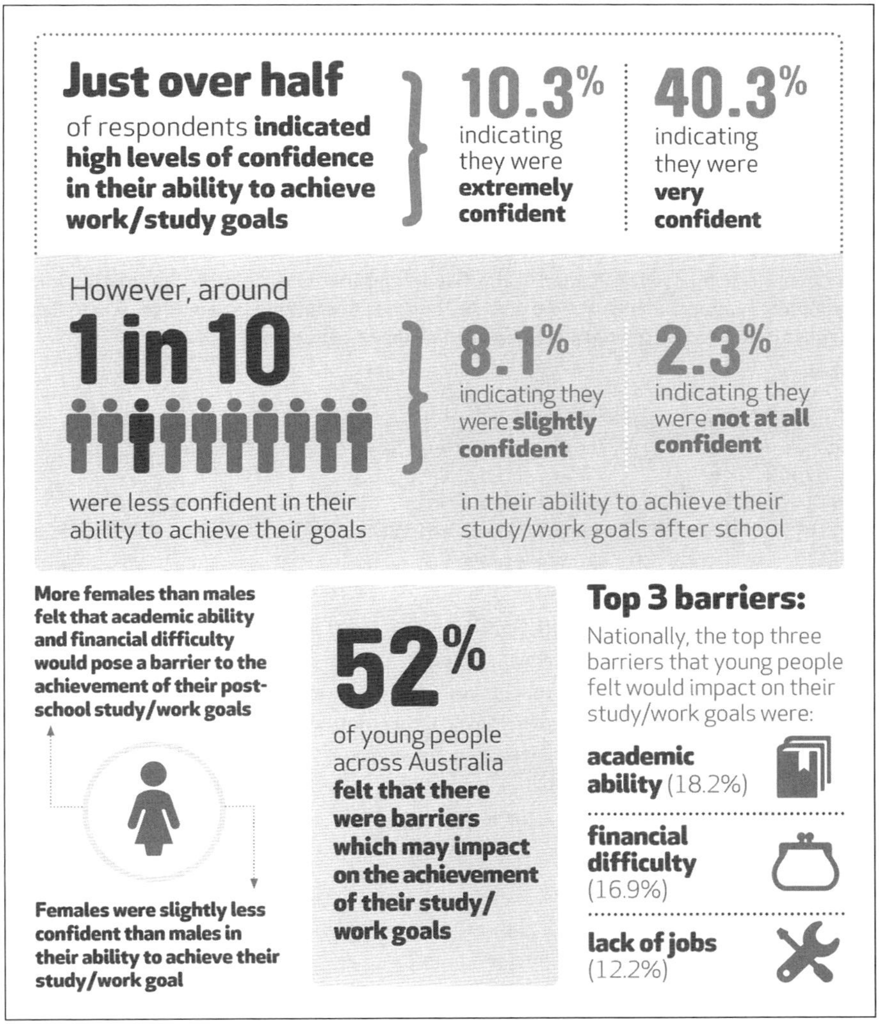

Source: Cave, L., Fildes, J., Luckett, G. and Wearring, A. 2015, Mission Australia's 2015 Youth Survey Report, *Mission Australia. © Mission Australia.*

a) Before you reply via email, collect information on the following items:
   - young Australians' concerns,
   - the matters they consider most important,
   - differences between female and male Australian teenagers' attitudes.

b) In an email of about 250 words, you then respond to the results of the study and also write about your concerns and issues you find important.

A letter to deal with the chocolate crisis

Basics

Sachlicher Brief

Sehr häufig werden Sie auf eine Aufgabenstellung stoßen, bei der Sie in Form eines Briefes einen Sachverhalt kommentieren sollen. Der Brief könnte beispielsweise an einen Freund / eine Freundin (persönlicher Brief) oder an eine Zeitung (Leserbrief) gerichtet sein.

Wie gehen Sie vor?

Bemühen Sie sich um eine übersichtliche Gliederung und eine sinnvolle Ausarbeitung Ihrer Argumente. Achten Sie auch auf die äußere Form des Briefes, indem Sie allgemeinen Regeln zum **Layout** folgen und gebräuchliche **Formulierungen** benutzen.

Layout

Briefkopf:	*Name and address*
Adresse des Empfängers / der Empfängerin:	*The Guardian Weekly* *Rockwood House* *9–17 Perrymount Rd.* *Haywards Heath RH16 3DH* *United Kingdom*
Datum:	October 15, 20 … / 15th October 20 …
Betreff:	*Your article "Child labour today"*
Anrede:	*Dear Sir or Madam*
Hauptteil (beginnt mit einem Großbuchstaben):	*I read your article "Child labour today" of October 15, 20 … with great interest and I would like to point out that …* *or: After reading your article …*
Schlussfloskel:	*Yours faithfully*
Unterschrift:	*Full name/Christian name only*

Formulierungen

Persönlicher Brief	Anrede	Schlussfloskel
• an eine(n) Freund(in)	*Dear Emma* *Dear Darren*	*Yours* *Love*
• an eine(n) Bekannte(n)	*Dear Mr Palmer* (UK) *Dear Mrs Palmer* (USA)	*Best wishes* *With best regards*
Leserbrief *(Letter to the Editor)*		
• an eine namentlich bekannte Person	*Dear Mr Sunberry* *Dear Miss Paull*	*Yours sincerely*
• an eine namentlich unbekannte Person	*Dear Sir or Madam* *Dear Sir (Madam)*	*Yours faithfully*

99 Your mother is still friends with her former exchange partner Amy Goodwill from York. Meanwhile, Amy has become head of the Consumer Service department at Lawson's Chocolate Factory and has arranged an internship for you so that you can improve your English. It is your job to prepare answers to letters of complaint and show them to Amy for approval afterwards. On your second day at work, you have to answer the following letter:

Mary Jane Smith
5 Filmer Road
Fulham
London SW6 7JE

Lawson's Chocolate Factory
Terry Lawson & Sons Limited
35 Auden Terrace
YORK YO2 5YE

24th July, 20 ...

Your confectionery "Lawson's Gold"

Dear Sir or Madam

I am very fond of your "Lawson's Gold" chocolates. For 45 years I have been a regular customer, and up to now I have never had any reason for complaint.

However, I must tell you that on opening the box I received today I was very disappointed. The chocolates didn't look at all fresh – in fact, they looked rather old and grey, which put me off tasting them. I have never come across a box of your chocolates in such poor condition before, so I felt I had to let you know, as the quality of your confectionery is usually of a superior standard.

Yours faithfully

Mary Jane Smith

Mary Jane Smith

a) Before you start writing an answer to this letter, you remember the key aspects of a suitable response to a complaint that Amy Goodwill has told you about:
   - Pay attention to the issue the customer addresses.
   - Give plausible reasons for what went wrong which do not put the company in an unfavourable light.
   - Offer some kind of compensation.

   Write two suitable sentences for each key aspect.

b) Then write a letter of about 100 words to Mary Jane Smith.

A blog entry on crossing the Alps in 7 days

Basics

Blogeintrag

Bei einem Blogeintrag kann es sich entweder um einen virtuellen Tagebucheintrag handeln oder um einen Kommentar bzw. eine Reaktion auf den Eintrag einer anderen Person, deren Ansichten man (nicht) teilt. Die Sprache ist generell **klar und prägnant** – **fassen Sie sich** also **kurz**. Bleiben Sie auch bei emotionalen Themen höflich und nutzen Sie eine **gehobene Sprachebene**. Gegenüber Gleichaltrigen könne Sie auch Umgangssprache verwenden. Vergessen Sie nicht, Ihrem Eintrag eine Überschrift, ein Datum sowie eine Uhrzeit zu geben.

100 You have recently become a member of the International Young Hikers' Community, which organises hiking trips in the Alps every summer. As your organisation is not very well-known yet, it has been decided that for each trip, one member has to make a contribution on the IYHC's weblog.
You have been asked to write an entry about your latest trip, which is a one-week tour across the Alps. You have already uploaded some photos for the blog entry.

a) Before you start writing, collect your impressions of each photo.

b) Then write a blog entry of 250 words that should motivate the readers to either join your group straightaway or to at least read other entries as well.

A letter to the editor on extreme advertising

Basics

Bildanalyse

In einem **Bild** oder einer **Karikatur** ist die Information verschlüsselt, d. h., was gesagt werden soll, wird nicht durch einen Text, sondern auf bildhafte Weise ausgedrückt. Ihre Aufgabe besteht darin, diese Aussage herauszuarbeiten. Ihre Lösung besteht aus zwei Teilen: der **Bildbeschreibung** und der **Interpretation**.

Wie gehen Sie vor?

Teil 1: **Bildbeschreibung** *(description)*

- Beschreiben Sie, was auf dem Bild / Cartoon zu sehen ist (Situation, Personen). Benutzen Sie das *simple present (The cartoon shows two people …)*.
- Beschreiben Sie, was geschieht und was die Personen tun (Handlung). Benutzen Sie die Verlaufsform *(The men are working on …)*.
- Beachten Sie eventuelle Bildunterschriften *(captions)* und Aussagen von Personen in Sprechblasen *(bubbles)*.

Teil 2: **Interpretation** *(message)*

- Halten Sie die Gesamtaussage fest *(The artist wants to show …)*.
- Versuchen Sie etwa vorhandene Bilder und Symbole zu entschlüsseln.
- Stellen Sie den Bezug her zwischen der dargestellten Situation und einer politischen oder gesellschaftlichen Situation bzw. Erscheinung.

Falls verlangt, kann sich auch ein 3. Teil anschließen, die persönliche Stellungnahme *(personal opinion)*.

Hilfreiche Wendungen:

The picture / cartoon shows …
In the picture / cartoon, you can see …
In the background … / in the foreground … / in the centre of the picture / cartoon …
On the left … / In the top right-hand corner you can see … / The left half shows …
The scene depicts …
The person on the left looks as if …
The picture / cartoon has a / no caption …
He / She / It stands for / represents / symbolises …
This indicates that …
It is obvious that …
The photographer / cartoonist illustrates … / wants to express the fact that …
The picture / cartoon is a reference to … / refers to … / is a criticism of …
The message of the cartoon is …
The picture / cartoon might suggest that …
This is an exaggerated view of …
To get this message across, the photographer / cartoonist …

101 You have bought a newspaper at the airport in Johannesburg, South Africa, on your way home from your holiday. On the plane, you read an article about the latest campaign of Feed SA, a South African non-governmental organisation, entitled "Abominably inappropriate advertising in South African supermarkets." The picture below is printed next to the article to underpin the journalist's view that these advertisements are "far beyond the pale as they manipulate guilt-ridden middle-class South Africans into donations". As you find the journalist's view highly inappropriate, you decide to write a letter to the editor as soon as you arrive home.

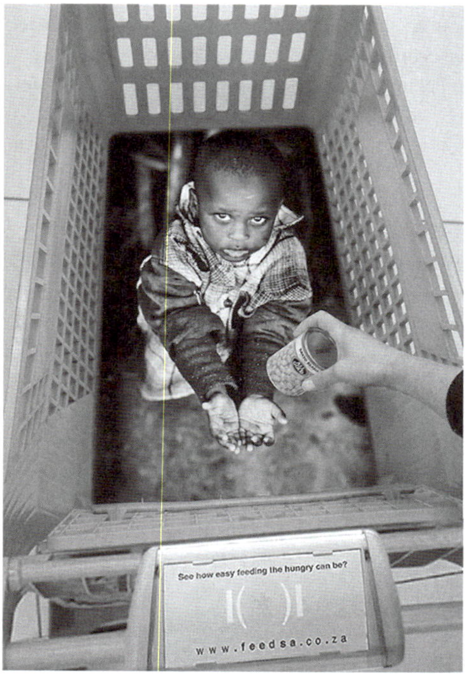

Source: http://adsoftheworld.com/sites/default/files/styles/media_retina/public/images/feedsatrolley.jpg?itok=cyCGOjTr

a) Use a maximum of 100 words to describe the picture.

b) Analyse the message of the picture and assess whether this kind of advertising is appropriate. Use five sentences each as a maximum.

c) Write a letter to the editor of about 250 words.

A cartoon analysis on environmental issues

102 You have to give a talk on the topic "How to deal with the environment in a responsible way" in your next English lesson and have decided to begin your speech with the cartoon below.

© *Welleman, Peter / Cartoonstock.com*

a) Describe the top section (above the water) and the lower section (under the water) of the cartoon briefly.

Above the water	Under the water

b) Explain the artist's message. Write about 120 words.

An analysis of statistics on teenage pregnancies

Basics

Diagramme und Statistiken

Diagrammarten

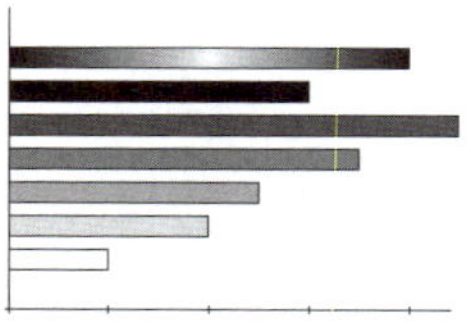

bar chart/graph
(Balken-, Säulendiagramm)

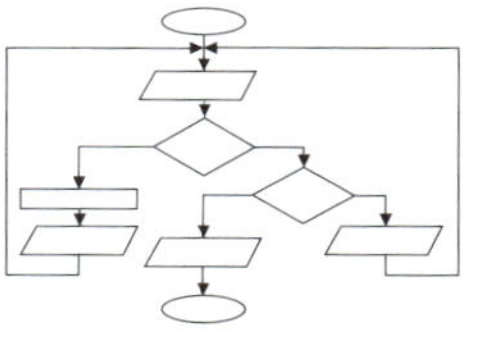

flow chart
(Flussdiagramm)

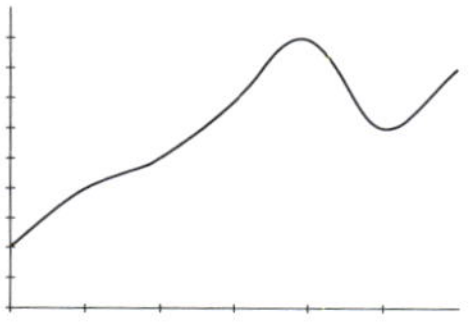

line graph
(Kurvendiagramm)

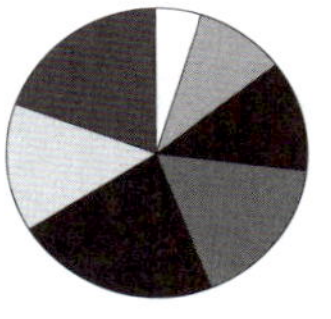

pie chart
(Kreisdiagramm, Kuchendiagramm)

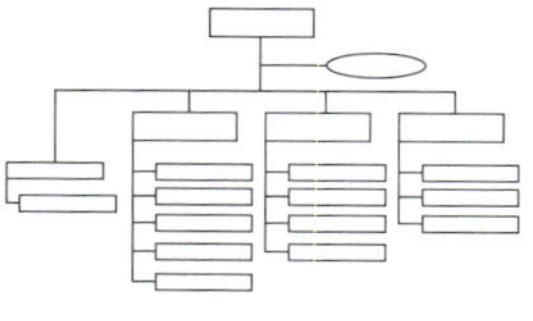

organisation(al) chart
(Organigramm)

Question	Answer
a) What are the conditions that would bring about multiculturalism in a positive sense according to the author?	• individual rights should be guaranteed to everyone • mutual respect of the individual groups
b) Which group makes it the most difficult to create a feeling of national identity?	white British people

table *(Tabelle)*

Hilfreiche Wendungen:

The pie chart shows / demonstrates / gives information about …
The bar chart compares …
Its most significant feature is …
The dotted line on the graph represents …
The figures prove that …
The statistics suggest that …
The diagram makes it clear that …
This implies that …
There is evidence that …

103 Your class has seen the film *Juno*, which is about a pregnant teenage girl in America. Now you have to do some research on the Internet concerning teenage pregnancies in the UK. In the course of your research, you have come across the following statistics.

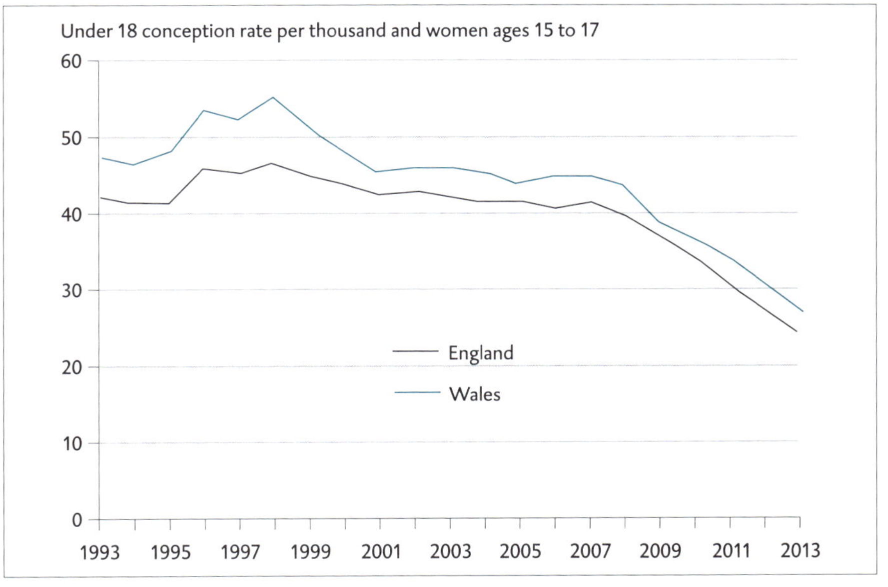

Source: Office for National Statistics: Conceptions in England and Wales, 2013.
Licensed under the Open Government Licence v.3.0.

a) List the approximate number of women aged 15 to 17 who were pregnant in the respective year and state the development of the graph in brackets.

Year	England (development)	Wales (development)
1998	47 per thousand (increase since 1997)	55 per thousand (considerable increase since 1997)
2001		
2006		
2013		

b) Interpret the message of the statistics. Write about 150 words.

A report on media usage

104 You are currently doing an internship at an international company that sells electronic devices. This week, it is your job to track the history of media usage in recent years. Today you have been given the following chart by your supervisor with the instruction to write a report on it.

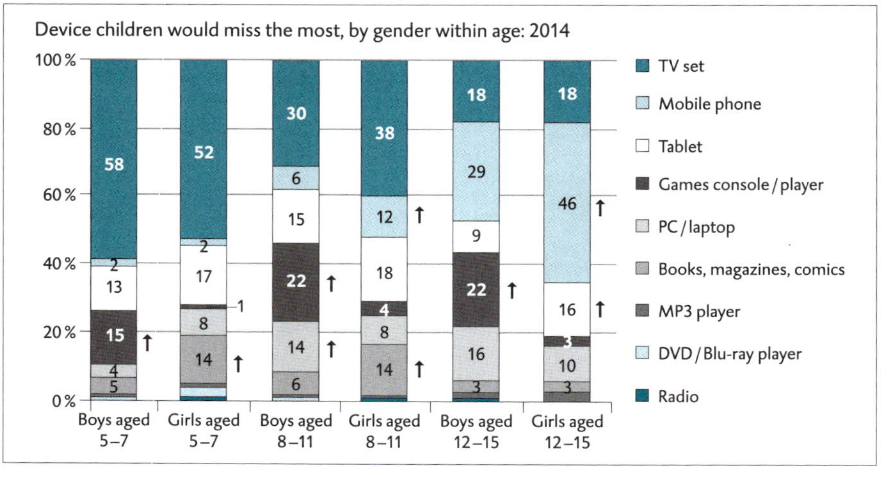

Quelle: Ofcom, in: Adults' Media Use and Attitudes Report 2014, *London: April 2014; page 23*

a) Complete the table with information about which device(s) boys and girls would have missed most in 2014. Fill in the grid below.

Level of necessity	Boys 5–7	Boys 8–11	Boys 12–15	Girls 5–7	Girls 8–11	Girls 12–15
most important						
fairly important (name 2)						
least important						

b) Write a report of about 200 words on the media usage of boys and girls aged 5 to 15 in the year 2014.

An application for a summer job

Basics

Bewerbung

Wenn Sie sich bei einer Firma per E-Mail bewerben, sollten Sie auf folgende Punkte achten.

Wie gehen Sie vor?

Bevor Sie die E-Mail schreiben:

- Lesen Sie sich die Ausschreibung ganz genau durch.
- Überprüfen Sie, ob Sie die geforderten Qualifikationen erfüllen.

Inhaltliche Aspekte:

- Beziehen Sie sich bereits in der **Einleitung** auf die Stellenausschreibung *(I am writing to express my interest in …)*.
- Führen Sie im **Hauptteil** aus, warum Sie für die Stelle geeignet sind (z. B. aufgrund Ihrer Ausbildung, Erfahrung oder Interessen).
- Geben Sie Referenzen an oder beziehen Sie sich auf Praktika *(work placement, internship)*, in denen Sie auf einem vergleichbaren Gebiet Erfahrungen sammeln konnten.
- Schließen Sie Ihre Ausführungen mit einer geeigneten **Schluss**formel (siehe Basics S. 134) und vergessen Sie nicht, Ihre vollständige Adresse inkl. E-Mail-Adresse anzugeben.

Formale Aspekte:

- Wählen Sie als Anrede „Dear Sir" oder „Dear Madam" bzw. den Namen des (der) verantwortlichen Mitarbeiters (Mitarbeiterin) in der Personalabteilung, falls dieser angegeben ist (siehe auch Basics S. 134).
- Nennen Sie in der Betreffzeile die Stelle, auf die Sie sich bewerben möchten, sowie Ihren vollständigen Namen.
- Achten Sie auf eine angemessene Sprache, also keine *short forms* oder umgangssprachliche Ausdrücke.

- Kontrollieren Sie, ob die Bewerbung vollständig ist und ob Sie die richtige E-Mail-Adresse angegeben haben.

105 You are looking for a summer job in an English-speaking country to improve your language skills. On the Internet, you have found the following job advertisement and decide to try your luck with an application.

a) List the main requirements and benefits of the summer job offered here.

b) E-mail Alistair Paull and send him an application of about 200 words telling him why you want to be involved and why you think you would be the right person for the job.

A comment on boarding schools

106 During your exchange to England, a heated discussion on boarding schools has taken place throughout the media, triggered by George Monboit, a journalist working for the British left-wing newspaper *The Guardian*.
In a video comment on *The Guardian's* website, Monboit claims:

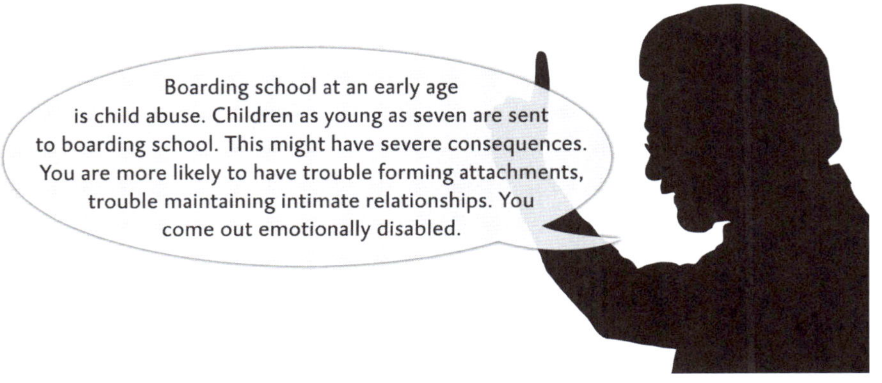

Source: George Monboit, on: www.theguardian.com, 11th February 2015

Back in Germany again, you decide to comment on Monboit's attitude on *The Guardian's* website.

a) Collect three aspects that either support or contradict George Monboit's point of view that boarding school at an early age is child abuse.

b) Write a comment of about 250 words.

Key

IDEA
ANALYSIS
MAIN
SUCCESS
Team
creative
Business
IDEA
IDEA

Reading

Teenagers at work

1

	A	Still more protection needed for working youngsters
5	B	Violation of laws against child labour
1	C	Current working regulations for young people
6	D	Jobs prevent teenage education
	E	Child labour in poorer countries
2	F	Long-term consequences of child labour in the past
3	G	Health hazards for child labourers
4	H	Efforts for the protection of working children

2

		true	false
a)	In the United States young people of 13 to 16 years of age may work up to three hours every day. **They are not allowed to work every day, but merely on school days.**	☐	☒
b)	Very often children work to become more financially independent.	☒	☐
c)	In the past, even very young children had to work to contribute to the family income.	☒	☐
d)	In the 19th century many working children were unable to read or write.	☒	☐
e)	Many accidents happened in the factories because children were not told about how dangerous machines could be. **They didn't obey the safety rules.**	☐	☒
f)	Charles Dickens and Karl Marx were two politicians who tried to improve the situation of working children. **Dickens was a writer, not a politician.**	☐	☒

g)	The new laws which limited the hours children were allowed to work were not respected by farmers and shop owners.	✗	
h)	Teenagers who work part-time learn to take care of themselves better.		✗

They are more likely to take drugs.

3

	Working young people in the past	**Working young people at present**
jobs	working in … • mines • factories • agriculture • shops	• doing a paper round • babysitting • washing cars • working as a waiter • working as a tutor • working in grocery stores • working as an actor • working as a model
age	from the age of 5 to 6 onwards	from the age of 14 to 16 onwards
working hours	13 to 16 hours a day	up to three hours on school days, but not after 7 p.m. and no more than 18 hours a week
hazards	• accidents • bad injuries • no education	• wasting money on drugs and drink (thus in danger of becoming addicted) • bad company • less time for study
measures taken or suggested	British legislation against child labour (1878)	hour restrictions

The darker side of fame

4 a) Kurt Cobain's mother …

- [ ] did not want her son to start a career as a musician.
- [ ] was surprised when she learned that Kurt had killed himself.
- [x] was always afraid that Kurt might commit suicide in the end.
- [ ] had no idea of the stress her son was under.

b) Kurt Cobain became involved with drugs because …

- [ ] it was the fashion of the time.
- [x] he was unhappy with his life.
- [ ] they helped him make better music.
- [ ] that was his way of rebelling against his parents.

c) With their music Cobain and his band …

- [x] expressed their protest against the adult world.
- [ ] showed their fans visions of a better future.
- [ ] wanted to earn as much money as possible.
- [ ] intended to create a new style of music.

d) Michael Jackson's career came to a halt when …

- [ ] he started taking drugs.
- [ ] the tyrannical behaviour of his father increased.
- [ ] the Jackson Five broke up.
- [x] rumours of sexual abuse were made public.

e) Michael Jackson earned particular fame because of his …

- [ ] strange appearance.
- [x] talents as a dancer and singer.
- [ ] frequent appearance in the media.
- [ ] special lifestyle.

f) It took Amy Winehouse some time to become famous because ...
- [ ] she was heavily addicted to drugs and could not perform well.
- [x] her first album was only noticed on a national level.
- [ ] she had a very difficult personality.
- [ ] she was not a mainstream singer.

g) What made Amy Winehouse's music special was ...
- [ ] her voice, which frequently cracked.
- [ ] her extraordinary performances on stage.
- [x] the combination of different styles of music.
- [ ] the topics she sang about.

5

1	2	3	4	5	6
D	E	B	A	F	C

6 a) People only know the stars and their lives from reports in the media, which nearly always show the glamour and the wealth celebrities enjoy. Thus, fans only get to hear the fairy tale side of being famous.

b) She meant that her son should not follow the example of some young celebrities who wasted their lives taking drugs and finally committed suicide.

c) Kurt Cobain and his band harshly criticised society and did not want to be a part of the rotten system they despised. But suddenly, they were celebrated and adored by members of that same society because of their songs. Thus, they did not know where they belonged anymore.

d) Michael Jackson changed his appearance through plastic surgery and his skin became increasingly white. Allegedly, this also influenced his character. He was accused of having abused young boys on his ranch. Drugs became his way of escaping from stress. In the end, he failed to overcome his addiction.

e) Amy Winehouse was unhappy in her marriage and alcohol and drugs became her way of escaping her sadness. Although she tried to stop drinking several times, she did not succeed.

f) Both Kurt and Amy were children from broken homes who rebelled against society in their teens and started taking drugs as a way of leaving their troubles behind. They both died aged 27.

Gap year "voluntourists"

7 The article …

- [ ] provides information on possibilities for young people working abroad.
- [x] summarises the findings of a study on voluntourism.
- [ ] warns about the negative effects of development aid.
- [ ] criticises the work of well-meaning volunteers in developing countries.

8 a) It has been held against "voluntourists" that they …
… cannot really help deprived people.

b) However, a new study found that the work of volunteers stimulates …
… sustainable development (within poor communities).

c) Thanks to young volunteers in Mozambique, an increasing number of AIDS patients were …
… taken care of at home.

d) Local communities as a whole benefit from the volunteers' …
… commitment/skills/willingness to take on work.

e) One negative effect of "voluntourism" is that locals …
… rely too much on volunteers/might not find work anymore.

f) To assess whether "voluntourism" is a real help for developing countries, one has to …
… measure its positive influence.

9

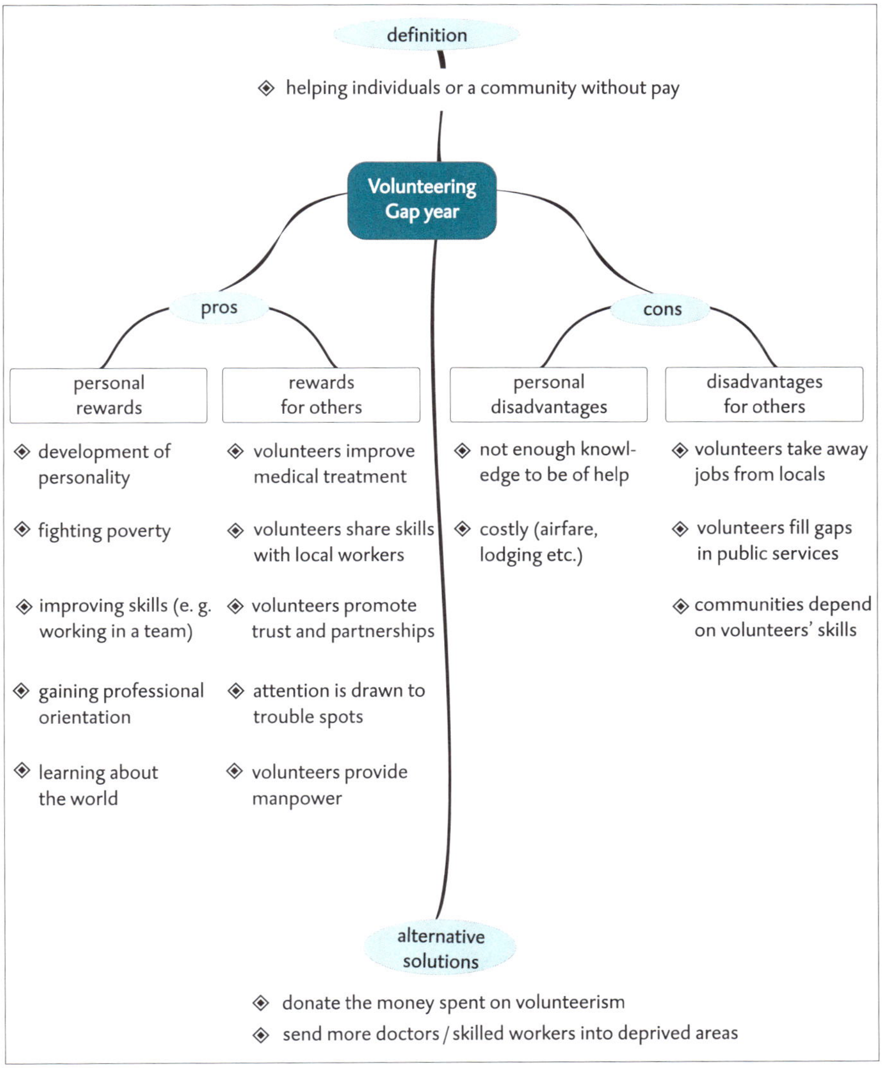
definition
helping individuals or a community without pay
Volunteering Gap year
pros
cons
personal rewards
rewards for others
personal disadvantages
disadvantages for others
development of personality
fighting poverty
improving skills (e. g. working in a team)
gaining professional orientation
learning about the world
volunteers improve medical treatment
volunteers share skills with local workers
volunteers promote trust and partnerships
attention is drawn to trouble spots
volunteers provide manpower
not enough knowl-edge to be of help
costly (airfare, lodging etc.)
volunteers take away jobs from locals
volunteers fill gaps in public services
communities depend on volunteers' skills
alternative solutions
donate the money spent on volunteerism
send more doctors / skilled workers into deprived areas

Micro stories

10

Micro Story	Latest Entry	Survival of the Fittest	Meeting People
Picture	B	C	F

11

Micro Story	Latest Entry	Survival of the Fittest	Meeting People
Alternative Headline	Delayed Post / Final Click / Final Countdown	From Top to Bottom / Superior Race / The End of the World as We Know It	Shop Talk / The Secret of Success / Up and Away /

12 a) The atmosphere in "Latest Entry" can be described as ...

- [x] pitiful and emotional.
- [ ] menacing and hostile.
- [ ] relaxed and exciting.

b) The setting of "Survival of the Fittest" can be referred to as ...

- [ ] lonely and cold.
- [x] spacious and vast.
- [ ] warm and welcoming.

c) The characters in "Meeting People" seem to be ...

- [ ] depressed and sad.
- [ ] majestic and mighty.
- [x] chatty and friendly.

13 The micro story "Latest Entry" is about a young woman who has prepared her **suicide**. However, before **leaving** for good, she wants to send a **message** to the world to let everyone know how badly she was treated and to take **revenge**. It is her wish to let everybody know who is to **blame** for what she had to do. However, because of a **technical** fault, the final posting cannot be distributed. Thus, sadly, nobody will ever get to know her side of the story.

"Survival of the Fittest" can be referred to as an illustration of Darwin's law: A new race, "the New Humans", is about to **get rid** of Mankind, the old race. Within a month a new deadly virus will **extinguish** the old breed and make room for a new superior species. The New Humans seem to be the **designers** of the lethal disease in order to create a new world. The means applied by the New Humans to reach their aim are as **brutal** as the ones used by Mankind. According to Darwin's theory of natural selection, the **triumph** of the new race is not the end of evolution, however. Sooner or later, the new rulers will be **replaced** by a more sophisticated species.

Eveline

14

Statement	a	b	c	d	e	f
Lines	ll. 3/4	ll. 8/9	ll. 13/14	ll. 16–18	ll. 23–25	ll. 32/33

15

appearance	hair tumbled forward, face of bronze, manly
character	outgoing, kind, open-hearted, caring, devoted to Eveline
hobbies	fond of music, likes to sing, goes to the theatre with Eveline

16

1	2	3	4	5
D	B	A	C	E

17

Reasons to leave with Frank 	• chance for a fresh start in Buenos Ayres in a home waiting for her • financial security through marriage with Frank • being in a relationship with a kind-hearted, generous and loving husband who treats her with respect • leaving a hard life with lots of responsibilities behind her • feeling of independence and promise of happiness
Reasons to stay 	• staying in familiar surroundings and with familiar people • breaking her promise to look after the family and the house • neglect of ageing father and younger children who depend on her • fear of what awaits her • the fact that she does not really love Frank

		true	false
18	a) Eveline is given special treats by Frank and enjoys his attention and kindness very much. Evidence: **Part I, ll. 13–18**	✗	☐
	b) Eveline had promised her sick mother to take care of the younger children as long as they needed her, which is why she feels guilty about leaving. Evidence: **Part I, ll. 30/31**	☐	✗
	c) Eveline had never been at sea before, which is why she worries herself sick. Evidence: **Part II, ll. 4–10**	☐	✗
	d) Eveline's feelings for Frank change when she identifies him as the cause for all her suffering. Evidence: **Part II, ll. 13/14**	✗	☐
	e) In her distressed state, Frank becomes a stranger to Eveline again. Evidence: **Part II, l. 21**	✗	☐

Father to son

19 a) Pictures A (present) and D (past)

b)

… father	• cannot talk to his son anymore • wants to know more about his son • does not share the same interests as his son • has tried hard to have a good relationship with his son • wants his son to regret the choices he has made • is angry about the current situation • wants to leave the misunderstandings behind
… son	• is trying to live his own life • seems willing to make up as well • has ideas and values that differ from his father's beliefs

20

☒	angry	☐	gloomy
☐	afraid	☐	indifferent
☒	desperate	☒	mad
☐	happy	☐	relieved
☐	hopeless	☒	sad

21 a) Have I destroyed the love (i. e. the father-son relationship) or formed it in the wrong place (i. e. where we have nothing in common)?

b) I wish he would come home again after having gone away, so that we could rebuild our relationship, rather than watch him live his own life./I would rather he return very poor, regretting the life he'd led, asking for help.

c) I would forgive him and start a new relationship in which love grows from the sadness.

d) We both try to reach out to each other but we find nothing to hold on to, no connection.

22 The **theme** of Elizabeth Jennings' poem, "Father to Son", is the generation gap. The **speaker** in the poem is a disappointed and frustrated father who mourns the loss of **contact** to his son. He admits that, despite having lived under the same roof for years, he does not really know anything about the interests, dreams and aspirations of his son now. To overcome the **estrangement**, he would like to rebuild a relationship with his son as it used to be when the boy was still young. In his **monologue**, the father asks himself whether he is responsible for the drifting apart. However, they do not communicate, and in a nostalgic **mood** the father wants his son to return home and be the friendly little boy again that he once was. He believes his son has done something wrong, because he says that he is ready to **forgive** him and start all over again.
The poem is composed of four **stanzas** with six lines each, with the **rhyme scheme** being a – b – b – a – b – a. The regular **form** suggests balance and harmony, but in reality the flow of speech is constantly interrupted by numerous **enjambments**. In this way the discrepancy between form and content mirrors the **conflict** of the two generations who live in different worlds. The father uses the **image** of the seed, which perhaps represents the love and affection which he has invested in his son. However, he is unable to understand

that he cannot much influence the growth of the plant. He does not realise that times have changed and that his son has developed his own **personality**.
All in all, Elizabeth Jennings makes the reader feel sorry for the father who is so deeply affected by the loss of communication with his son but, at the same time, she shows that it is not always the children's **fault** when parents and the younger generation distance themselves from each other.

Listening

Gun possession

Track 1

Transcript of Podcast from Youthradio

When I was 12 something happened that made me think buying a gun wasn't the worst idea. I thought it could give me what I would like to call, "a twisted peace of mind".
One morning I was on my way to the bus stop when I heard gunshots. I looked back and saw no one. Then out of nowhere I spotted a guy running towards me, wearing a grey sweat suit with a gun in his hand. I took off in the opposite direction. As I was running I saw someone on the ground, across the street. It was my teenage cousin, lying in a pool of his own blood.
Growing up in West Oakland, I've witnessed robberies, drug deals and even people being paid to commit murder. It wasn't unusual to see my older cousins load their guns before going to the corner store to buy some eggs and milk. Wearing a gun seemed as essential as wearing a pair of boxers. There have been plenty of times when I've had the money and the right connections to purchase a fire arm.
But each time, at the last minute, I stop and think to myself, "Do I honestly need a gun?" Then I'd buy a pair of shoes instead.
My friends asked me things like, "Why don't you tote? You're too scared to get a hammer?" and quite frankly the answer is yes. I'm scared of losing my freedom. I'm scared of the effect the gun could have on my personality. And I'm scared of the thought of ending a person's life.
Thankfully my grandparents and I relocated from West Oakland to a much calmer neighbourhood. For the first time I was free to think more about music, sports and shoes, without those thoughts being drowned out by drama.
Every now and then I still find myself in a potentially threatening situation, and I start to think about getting a gun. But then I remember buying a piece would only ruin the peace I already have. With a perspective, I'm Jahlil Jackson. [...]

Source: By Jahlil Jackson for Youth Radio, © Youth Radio

23 a) When Jahlil Jackson was 12, he ...

- [ ] saw how a man was shot at the bus stop.
- [ ] held a gun in his hands for the first time.
- [x] first thought about buying a gun.
- [ ] was threatened by a gunman.

b) Jahlil Jackson saw a man running towards him, so he ...

- [ ] hid inside the corner store.
- [ ] attempted to stop him.
- [x] tried to get away as quickly as possible.
- [ ] called the police.

c) In the past, Jahlil Jackson ...

- [x] could easily have bought a gun.
- [ ] did not know the right people to buy a gun.
- [ ] did not have enough money to purchase a gun.
- [x] thought it essential to possess a gun.

d) Jahlil Jackson had his doubts about buying a gun as he was scared ...

- [x] of a change of character.
- [ ] of having to actually use it.
- [x] that he might end up being a murderer.
- [ ] of coming to contact with the wrong kind of people.

e) Jahlil Jackson was happy that ...

- [ ] his family moved to another state.
- [x] his grandparents moved to a less dangerous neighbourhood.
- [ ] his family moved to another city.
- [ ] he could leave his former neighbourhood for college.

f) In his new surroundings, Jahlil ...

- [ ] feels completely safe.
- [x] can focus on more everyday issues.
- [ ] does not need a gun anymore.
- [x] experiences less hardship and violence.

24 a) Jahlil Jackson grew up in a very rough neighbourhood amidst robbers, drug dealers and killers. Wearing a gun was not only regarded as normal but essential. Gunfights in the streets were frequent, and one day Jahlil saw how his cousin was shot.

b) To Jahlil's cousins, carrying a gun is as normal and essential as going to the supermarket. Only wearing a gun will earn you respect and the ability to defend yourself.

c) Jahlil's friends thought that he was a coward, too afraid of wearing a gun.

d) Violence causes worries and makes it impossible to think about the good and pleasant sides of life (e. g. music, sports, clothes).

British politicians on immigration

Theresa May on immigration

Track 2

Transcript

There are millions of people in poorer countries who would love to live in Britain, and there is a limit to the amount of immigration any country can and should take. While we must fulfil our moral duty to help people in desperate need, we must also have an immigration system that allows us to control who comes to our country.

Because when immigration is too high, when the pace of change is too fast, it's impossible to build a cohesive society. It's difficult for schools and hospitals and core infrastructure like housing and transport to cope. And we know that for people in low-paid jobs, wages are forced down even further, while some people are forced out of work altogether.

Now I know there are some people who say, yes there are costs of immigration, but the answer is to manage the consequences, not reduce the numbers. But not all of the consequences can be managed, and doing so for many of them comes at a high price.

We need to build 210,000 new homes every year to deal with the rising demand. We need to find 900,000 new school places by 2024. And there are thousands of people who have been forced out of the labour market, still unable to find a job.

But even if we could manage all the consequences of mass immigration, Britain does not need net migration in the hundreds of thousands every year. Of course, immigrants plug skills shortages and it's right that we should try to attract the best talent in the world, but not every person coming to Britain right now is a skilled electrician, engineer or doctor.

The evidence – from the OECD, the House of Lords Economic Affairs Committee and many academics – shows that while there are benefits of selective and controlled immigration, at best the net economic and fiscal effect of high immigration is close to zero. So there is no case, in the national interest, for immigration of the scale we have experienced over the last decade.

Source: www.independent.co.uk, 6th October 2015

25

		true	false
a)	Millions of people from poorer countries have come to live in Britain.	☐	☒
b)	Theresa May wants to reduce the number of newcomers through stricter entry requirements.	☒	☐
c)	The rapidly increasing numbers of immigrants challenge the stability of British society.	☒	☐
d)	The most urgent measures in the years to come will be to provide housing and jobs for the immigrants.	☐	☒
e)	The country is already confronted with a high unemployment rate.	☒	☐
f)	The priority is for Britain to accept academic immigrants whose skills are in demand.	☐	☒
g)	May's tough stand on immigration is based on findings of the OECD and the House of Commons.	☐	☒

26

Summary	Errors
Theresa May predicts that ~~310,000~~ new housing facilities will have to be built ~~next~~ year to meet the increasing demand. In addition, ~~90,000~~ places more will be needed in schools by the year ~~2020~~.	210,000 every 900,000 2024

David Cameron on immigration

Track 3

Transcript

If you have uncontrolled immigration, you have uncontrolled pressure on public services. And that raises basic issues of fairness. Uncontrolled immigration can damage our labour market and push down wages. And working people rightly want a government that's on their side. Uncontrolled immigration means too many people coming to the UK legally but staying illegally. And people are fed up with a system that allows those who are not meant to be in our country to remain here. So the British people want these things sorted. And as the Home Secretary's just said, we've been working over the last five years towards that. We've fundamentally taken the approach that we inherited and changed it.

Bogus colleges – they've been shut down. Paying the rent and dole of jobless migrants – we've stopped that. Illegal immigrants driving on our roads – we revoked their licences – over 9,000 of them. People from outside Europe using the NHS for free – we're now charging them and putting the money back into our health service.
And we've clamped down on the fake brides and grooms entering into sham marriages; we brought in exit checks so we will know who is here, and whether they should have gone home, and we also said to all parts of government: controlling immigration isn't just a job for the Home Office – it's a job for health, for employment, housing, education, business, the treasury – everyone. It's what I call a whole government approach.

Source: Prime Minister pledges to control and reduce immigration. Prime Minister's Office, 10 Downing Street: Press Release, 21st May 2015.

27 If you have uncontrolled immigration, you have uncontrolled **pressure** on public services. And that raises basic issues of fairness. Uncontrolled immigration can **damage** our labour market and push down wages. And working people rightly want a government that is on their **side.** Uncontrolled immigration means too many people coming to the UK **legally** but staying illegally. And people are fed up with a system that allows those who are not **meant** to be in our country to remain here. So the British people want these things **sorted**. And as the Home Secretary's just said, we've been working over the last five years towards that. We've fundamentally taken the **approach** that we inherited and changed it.

28

29

A	B	C	D	E
5	1	2	3	4

Food policy report

Track 4

Transcript

Report: Conflict, Climate Affect Food Security
by Joe DeCapua

A new report says there were both advances and setbacks in food security in 2014. Poverty was reduced last year and the number of hungry people declined. However, conflict, climate change and disease disrupted food production and trade.
The International Food Policy Research Institute has released its Global Food Policy Report. IFPRI Director-General Shenggen Fan lists some of the accomplishments of last year.
"We have achieved some progress. For example, we paid more attention to nutrition. We also think water, hygiene are very important in solving children's under-nutrition. We have also seen new commitments on trade and the climate change – and a focus on family farming. The year 2014 was a year of family farming. So we made enough progress on various fronts."
But Fan said 2014 had its share of threats to food security. "For example, persistent conflicts, re-emerging of zoonotic diseases – avian influenza, Ebola – and continued extreme weather shocks – typhoons in the Philippines – rising food safety scandals – Taiwan, mainland China and beyond. Higher prices of nutritious foods, such as vegetables and the fruits, despite very stable grain prices for the last four or five years."
Syria topped the list of conflicts in 2014 with its regional impact. Somalia and South Sudan are other examples of how conflict threatens food security for millions of people.
"We have seen the increased correlation between conflicts and increased malnutrition in many parts of the world. In the rest of the world, we have achieved tremendous progress in cutting hunger and malnutrition, although the number is still very high. But it is in some of the conflict zones that malnutrition is actually rising," he said.
Fan said climate change has long-term consequences on food security. He says there are still some skeptics, despite the overwhelming number of studies confirming its effects.

"Increased floods, cyclones, droughts definitely should change their mind. And extreme weather events will happen more frequent [sic] and more extreme [sic]. That will affect the ability of human beings in producing more food and more nutritious food."
The Global Food Policy Report says conditions for thousands of people fleeing violence in northern Nigeria, Central African Republic and Mali were made worse by low rainfall and drought. It says that a "lack of rain threatened the food and nutrition security and livelihoods of both hosting communities and refugees."
The report adds the occurrence of both weather shocks and conflicts may not be coincidental saying that abnormally high temperatures in Sudan and South Sudan strongly raise the risk of conflict.
The IFPRI Director-General said lessons about food security were learned during the Ebola crisis: "The first lesson we learned is our global food system is very vulnerable to diseases. Ebola has [a] huge impact on people's access to nutritious food. The production was interrupted. The market was disrupted. The trade does not come. For example, some of the rice-exporting countries were very reluctant to send their grains to the Ebola-affected countries."
The International Food Policy Research Institute also said middle income countries play a pivotal role in eliminating hunger and malnutrition. It said while Brazil, China, India, Indonesia and Mexico may be "rising economic powerhouses", middle income countries are home to more than 360 million hungry people.
"They are facing [a] triple burden of malnutrition. Hunger – 50 percent of the world's hungry people live in these countries. Then, lack of micronutrients – Vitamin A, zinc, iron, and also increased obesity and overweight. So, they are facing triple burdens and the second burden, third burden arising very quickly."
The IFPRI report called on governments of middle income countries to "reshape their food systems to focus on nutrition and health, closing the gender gap in agriculture and improving rural infrastructure."
Fan says the report will be used to influence the writing of the Sustainable Development Goals. They'll soon succeed [sic] the Millennium Development Goals. There could be as many as 17 SDGs compared to eight for the MDGs, and they could contain nearly 170 target areas. Joe DeCapua, VOA News, Washington.

Joe DeCapua: Report: Conflict, Climate Affect Food Security. In: Voice of America News, 19th March, 2015

30 a) Shenggen Fan states that many children …

- ☐ have become refugees.
- ☒ do not have enough to eat.
- ☐ do not receive proper medical care.
- ☐ are exploited on their parents' farms.

b) The Global Food Policy Report reveals that there is a connection between …

- [ ] progress and a decrease in malnutrition.
- [x] trouble spots and an increase in hunger.
- [ ] food security and a increase in population.
- [ ] food security and a decrease in malnutrition.

c) To illustrate climate change the director mentions:

- [x] floods.
- [ ] hurricanes.
- [ ] heat waves.
- [x] droughts.

d) Diseases such as Ebola influence the global food system as they bring about a …

- [x] decrease in production.
- [x] change of trade routes.
- [ ] different attitude to how food is selected.
- [x] confusion of the market.

e) "Middle income countries" play a crucial role in the global food system because there, people …

- [x] eat food that lacks important ingredients.
- [x] eat in an unbalanced way.
- [ ] develop eating disorders.
- [x] still do not have enough to eat.

31 a) When it comes to children's diet, hygiene …
… plays a crucial role.

b) The more conflicts there are in a country, the more people …
… starve/go hungry/are underfed/have nothing to eat.

c) Due to climate change the production of food …
… will decline/will decrease.

d) Refugees in African countries were particularly affected by …
… low rainfall and drought/lack of rain.

32

- [ ] During the Ebola crisis, many countries were reluctant to take in grain from abroad.
- [ ] In middle income countries, there are still billions of people suffering from malnutrition.
- [X] Weight problems and deficient diets will become an even bigger problem in these countries in the future.
- [X] Middle income countries also need to take efforts to better the situation of people living and working in rural areas.

From a teenager's perspective:

Nanette Thompson talks about being an only child

Track 5

Transcript of Podcast from Youthradio

Growing up as an only child, my friends always told me how lucky I was. "My bratty brother won't stop taking my stuff," they would say. They told me they wished they were only kids too. I would nod politely, but in my heart I was jealous. I'm Nanette Thompson with a commentary for Youthradio.

As long as I could remember, I wanted a sister I could share secrets with – a biological partner in crime. I fantasized about the trouble we would get into, and the arguments and rivalries we'd have. But as I – and my parents – got older, it became clear that I was going to stay an only child.

And there are benefits. Time to myself, having my own room, and no hand-me-downs. Still I can't help but feel some sibling rivalry could have better prepared me for life. My child-hood is coming to a close. But I may actually get a second chance for siblings. Next fall when I go off to college I hope to join a sorority. And if things go as planned, I will have what I always wanted – sisters. And maybe a little rivalry. For Youthradio, I'm Nanette Thompson.

Source: By Nanette Thompson for Youth Radio, © Youth Radio

33

	true	false	not given
a) Nanette's friends envied her that she did not have any brothers and sisters.	X		
b) She herself was quite happy to grow up as an only child.		X	
c) Nanette's parents decided to have only one child for financial reasons.			X

d) She is looking forward to having "sisters" at college.	☒	☐	☐
e) Nanette hopes that there will be no trouble between the girls in the sorority.	☐	☒	☐

34

advantages of being an only child	advantages of having brothers and sisters
• time to oneself • no hand-me-downs • nobody to share possessions with / having one's own room	• somebody to share secrets with ("partner in crime") • lots of adventures and common experiences • rivalry prepares you better for life

Teaching tech to mom by Nanette Thompson

Track 6

Transcript of Podcast from Youthradio

I remember when my mom taught me my ABC's and how to make spaghetti – but now that everyone is addicted to their smartphones, our roles are reversed. Now I'm the teacher. I am Nanette Thompson with a commentary for Youthradio.

I was twelve when I learned how to make a Powerpoint. My mom was 50. She was applying for a new job, and she wanted to add visuals. I sat next to her, taking over the mouse as she pointed out the fonts she wanted, the colors, the pictures.

That was six years ago, and I'm still showing her how to do certain things like attach documents to her emails and add emojis to her text messages.

Although this process is frustrating, my mom is teaching me patience, how to work with different personalities in what feels like a job setting. And while technology comes easy to me, having to teach my mom the basics has made me understand how I learn.

Next year, I'm heading off to college, which means my mom will need to figure out her technology issues for herself. I'm pretty sure she'll be fine … but if not, I'm just a cell phone call away. For Youthradio, I'm Nanette Thompson.

Source: By Nanette Thompson for Youth Radio, © Youth Radio

35 a) Nanette Thompson taught her mother how to …

- ☐ use her smartphone.
- ☒ work with Powerpoint.
- ☐ use the computer.

b) She thinks that her mother is …
- [ ] making progress fast.
- [x] still slow on the computer.
- [ ] an almost hopeless case.

c) Nanette claims that teaching technology to her mother …
- [ ] has been a disillusioning experience.
- [x] has given her a deeper insight into the learning process itself.
- [ ] will not be an issue anymore as soon as she is off to college.

36 a) As a digital native, Nanette knew how to work with computer **programmes** although she was only **12** years old.

b) She helped her mum with a job **application**.

c) Her mother told her which fonts and colours to use by **pointing** to them.

d) Nanette's mother still struggles with **attaching** documents to emails or **adding** emojis to text messages.

e) Through her teaching Nanette learned how to be more **patient**.

The age of smartphones

Teenagers and smartphone addiction

Track 7

Transcript

SCOTT SIMON, Host: Give evolution a chance and humans may grow a third arm and eye – to look at our screens. People cross the street these days and never look up from their smartphones. Try talking to a teenager whose eyes don't wander to their tablet. Groups from churches to schools to gyms now hold digital cleanses for people to try to survive without screen time for a weekend or so. Tony Gonzalez of member station WPLN was on the scene when 42 Nashville students turned in their phones and when they got them back.

TONY GONZALEZ, Byline: The clock is ticking for Maplewood High students Destiny Davis and Jamya Whitmore. They're about to give up their cell phones for 24 hours. They clutch them as they get mentally prepared. Davis says the good part will be talking to her family more. And the bad part, kind of the same.

DESTINY DAVIS: Because we're always communicating on our phone. Like, your family could be in the next room, and we're texting them, but now you have to get up and walk and go get them *(laughter)*.

GONZALEZ: Then it gets real. Teacher Jarred Amato gives the five-minute warning.
JARRED AMATO: Put up a picture on Instagram.
GONZALEZ: Their last Facebook updates and Snapchats for the next 24 hours.
AMATO: Say goodbye. Five minutes – five minutes and I'm going to start to pick them up.
DESTINY: What? I thought I've got five minutes.
JAMYA WHITMORE: She already can't go without her phone. That's sad.
DESTINY: *(Laughter)* Five minutes.
JAMYA: How we going to live? I need my phone.
DESTINY: Oh, my God.
GONZALEZ: The girls put their phones in Ziploc bags. Then, it's time for the group to take a pledge about technology addiction.
WHOLE GROUP: We are spending more time communicating with our screens than with each other.
GONZALEZ: Single file, they stack their phones in a cardboard box. Some even kiss them goodbye.
UNIDENTIFIED STUDENT: Bye, baby.
GONZALEZ: Yes, that student just said, "Bye, baby". The phones will spend the night locked in a cabinet. This attachment between students and their phones is nothing less than addiction, says Amato, an English teacher still in his twenties. He relates to his students about the awesome power of smartphones, but he at least remembers a world before they were in every pocket all the time.
AMATO: There's always a text message to send. There's always a new picture to see. There's always a new Snapchat to send, that they never get a break. And if you ask them, they really don't like it, but they almost feel powerless to it.
GONZALEZ: Fast forward to the next morning. Amato senses something different in his classroom. It's louder because the kids are talking and making eye contact. Destiny and Jamya are comparing how much extra sleep they got without their phones around.
DESTINY: I went to sleep at 11, looking for my phone …
JAMYA: No TV, no phone, no nothing.
DESTINY: And I was just bored after that. I don't care. I was bored.
GONZALEZ: By morning, she felt something unusual.
DESTINY: I was ready to get to school to get my phone *(laughter)*. If the bus could just move a little faster *(laughter)*.
GONZALEZ: To milk the moment, the teacher asks a few more questions as the phones sit just out of reach. Most say unplugging is easier than expected. Several played outside for the first time in a while. And then, at long last, they tear the bags open.
AMATO: One, two, three. […]
GONZALEZ: First order of business, count the missed messages, likes, Snapchats and Kiks.
JAMYA: Got one from Facebook, six from Kik, two from regular message, seven from ooVoo.
GONZALEZ: ooVoo, that's a video calling app. It turns out the group was missing messages, but they were still there, waiting to be read, after everyone had unplugged to live a little. For NPR News, I'm Tony Gonzalez in Nashville.

Source: Tony Gonzalez: Screen-Free For A Day, Teens Try Life Without Phones. In: NPR, November 7, 2015.

37 a)

reporter	student	teacher
Tony Gonzalez	Destiny Davis	Jarred Amato
	Jamya Whitmore	

b) The report is about an experiment which requires students to …

- [ ] do without screen time for a week.
- [x] give up their smartphones for a day.
- [ ] take part in a digital cleanse for a weekend.

The students are …

- [ ] totally against the experience.
- [ ] excited about the experience.
- [x] unsure and nervous.

Jarred Amato believes that students are …

- [x] constantly occupied with their smartphones.
- [ ] desperate to get away from their phones.
- [x] unable to fight their smartphone addiction.

It turns out that without their phones, students have …

- [x] the urge to talk to each other much more.
- [x] slept more hours than usual.
- [ ] spent more time with their families.

38

Dialog	Errors
Like Destiny Davis, some students felt ~~good~~ when they were not receiving any messages. For ~~half~~ of them, unplugging was easier ~~then~~ expected. Several spent time ~~inside~~ the family home, which had not happened for a ~~month~~ at least. It might be a consolation to some that the missed ~~calls~~ are still there on the phones to be ~~received~~.	bored most than outside while messages read

The fear of being out of phone contact

Track 8

Transcript

Do you ever receive phantom phone messages, imagining sounds or vibrations from your pocket? Do you sleep with your phone within arms' reach like 90 per cent of under 30s? You might like more than half of Britons suffer from nomophobia, anxiety of being out of phone contact. Your body is trying to tell you something – and it's not good news. If your phone is switched on, the very act of not checking it puts you under pressure, your brain is unconsciously eager to handle your device, and suppressing this takes effort. In a famous 1996 experiment psychologist Roy Baumeister allowed some volunteers to eat a display of freshly baked cookies, but others were told to resist temptation. Later those who had resisted gave up more than twice as quickly as the others when faced with a difficult task. They simply had less willpower left. We've seen this result time and time again. The very act of resisting temptation takes a toll, and this matters a great deal when it comes to technology. Are your unread emails hovering in a background browser tab? This reduces your effective IQ by 10 points. Your mind literally has fewer resources to spare. Technology isn't toxic, your phone is not a brain cigarette, and nor are most of us addicts. But it is seductive and calibrated to entice. Facebook, Instagram and Twitter are casinos. Your time is their money. Just one more click, another "like", another "link". But here's the thing. You're pricing yourself too cheap. Your willpower, your attention – these are limited resources and others are only too good at spending them for you. Consider multitasking – a word invented to describe what computers do. Human brains can't actually multitask. At MIT, research by Earl Miller and others has shown that what we really do is switch rapidly between tasks. We get instant gratification from accomplishing something; a tiny email, a link clicked, while we steadily become less effective. Like a punter playing a slot machine we start to need the short-term rush while the long-term slips out of view. When faced with a difficult question, writes Nobel laureate Daniel Kahneman, we often answer an easier one instead, usually without noticing the substitution. Don't let your life become a series of answers to questions that aren't worth answering. Demand a great relationship with tech by spending at least a little time apart.

Source: Louis van Kleef, Leah Green, Tom Chatfield; on: www.theguardian.com, 4th November 2015

39 Best summary: **B**

40

1	2	3	4	5	6
E	C	D	A	F	B

Dating habits

British people's dating habits

Track 9

Transcript

It is estimated that one in five new relationships and one in six marriages now begins online. A recent study found that marriages that start online are 25 % more likely to last than those between couples who met through more traditional means. And while a third of people surveyed in 2005 described online dating as "desperate", that figure has dropped to less than a fifth today. Since dating juggernaut match.com launched back in 1995 more than 75 million people have logged onto the service which is accessible in 40 countries. Men on the site tend to work in engineering, finance and retail, while women are most commonly secretaries, doctors and teachers. When creating a profile certain words are more likely to buy you a date. Try name checking yoga, dog, surf, comedy and explore. Oh, and use smiley faces, especially ones with noses.

Source: Sarah Rainey, Lauren Alpe; on: www.telegraph.co.uk, 11th February 2015

41 a) Relationships of people who have met online are ...

- [ ] less stable than those of partners who have met offline.
- [x] more stable than those of partners who have met offline.
- [ ] as stable as those of partners who have met offline.

b) Since 2005, people's attitude to online dating has ...

- [ ] not changed at all.
- [x] become more positive.
- [ ] become more negative.

c) Match.com is a leading online dating service which ...

- [ ] is represented in over 50 countries.
- [x] is used by over 70 million people.
- [ ] was launched at the beginning of the 21st century.

d) Most people who use online dating services work in ...

- [ ] jobs that require a lot of travelling.
- [ ] the industrial sector.
- [x] jobs that require a high level of education.

e) A successful profile contains words like ...
- [ ] dog, soda, comedy.
- [ ] explore, chat, yoga.
- [x] yoga, comedy, dog.

42 It is estimated that one in five new relationships and one in **six** marriages now begins online. A recent study found that marriages that start online are **25 %** more likely to **last** than those between couples who met through more traditional means. And while a **third** of people surveyed in **2005** described online dating as "desperate", that figure has **dropped** to less than a **fifth** today. Since dating juggernaut match.com launched back in **1995** more than **75** million people have logged onto the service which is accessible in **40** countries.

Source: Sarah Rainey, Lauren Alpe; on: www.telegraph.co.uk, 11th February 2015

American teens' dating habits

Track 10

Transcript

ROBERT SIEGEL, Host: Teenagers, love and technology – we know those things are all linked. And today, a new study by the Pew Research Center shows how much. The survey finds half of teenagers ages 13 to 17 have let someone know they have feelings for them through social media sites such as Facebook. NPR's Brakkton Booker reports that while only a small percentage say that they've met a significant other online, social media play an important role in maintaining romances.

BRAKKTON BOOKER, Byline: Before jumping into the complicated world of teenage love with all the likes and posts and re-tweets, I thought I should get up to speed. Washington D.C.'s Chinatown Metro stop is a popular spot where teens hang out after school. Fifteen-year-old Skye Crutchfield and Jewell Sutton explain to me just how people their age let others know they are single.

JEWELL SUTTON: Put that in your bio.

SKYE CRUTCHFIELD: Yeah, you put it in your bio. You're, like, single, and – you know?

JEWELL: Or you put the emoji that's unlocked.

BOOKER: Stefan McPherson and Phillip White agree. Emojis are where it's at if you're in a serious relationship.

UNIDENTIFIED TEEN: Yeah *(unintelligible)*. You probably just put down a little, like, a hearty emoji and then, like, the @name.

BOOKER: The Pew study "Teens, Technology and Romantic Relationships" found social media is a top venue for flirting. But while less than 10 per cent say they've met a significant other online, just about two thirds say social media helps them feel connected to a boyfriend or girlfriend. And lead researcher, Amanda Lenhart, learned emojis are vitally important.

AMANDA LENHART: The hand-holding, the padlock and the heart emojis seem to be the most critical, at least in the focus groups that we conducted.
BOOKER: Lenhart said she was surprised sixty-five per cent of boys said social media makes them feel closer to a romantic partner compared to just over half of teenage girls.
LENHART: They're more likely to say they felt an increased emotional connection and an increased kind of just connection in general to those workings of their partners' lives.
BOOKER: While teens are certainly on Facebook, Lenhart says it's not where they go to flirt or maintain relationships. Like, "Duh, your mom is on Facebook. Hello?!" Lenhart says teens tend to gravitate to visually oriented sites like Snapchat and Instagram. But when it comes to breakups, she says, surprisingly, it's still done the old-fashioned way – in person.
LENHART: That's the most socially acceptable way to break up with somebody, but it's not considered to be particularly socially acceptable to dump somebody on – by text, but a lot of people do it.
BOOKER: And of course, once that's done, the pruning or deleting of pictures and blocking exes and changing your social media profile ensues. Laurence Steinberg teaches psychology at Temple University, and he's also the author of "Age Of Opportunity: Lessons From The New Science Of Adolescence." Steinberg says today's teens are not that much different than previous generations. Sometimes they pick a boyfriend or girlfriend to gain admiration of their peers. And he adds this study should help parents' angst about what their teens are doing on social media.
LAURENCE STEINBERG: I think a lot of adults today have unnecessary worries about the ways in which social media are disrupting adolescents' emotional development. And I think social media are – they're not the evil that many people think of them as.
BOOKER: Many teens may favourite that sentiment. Brakkton Booker, NPR News, Washington.

43

A	B	C	D	E
4	1	5	2	3

44

	true	false	not given
a) Social media play an important role in starting romances.	☐	☒	☐
b) Chinatown Metro stop in Washington is a popular place for teenagers to meet after school.	☒	☐	☐
c) The emojis used indicate how serious a relationship is.	☐	☐	☒

d) Though few teenagers have met their current partner online, social media is used for flirting a lot.	☒	☐	☐
e) Facebook is the preferred site for teenagers to flirt or maintain relationships.	☐	☒	☐
f) The number of adults having an account with Snapchat or Instagram is rising.	☐	☐	☒
g) An increasing number of teenagers pick their partner to gain admiration from their peers.	☐	☒	☐
h) Parents should worry less about what their teens are doing on social media.	☒	☐	☐

Mediation

Mit beiden Beinen im Salat

45 a) Information concerning ...

- **the person portrayed:** Maurice Maggi, aged 58, lives in Zurich. He comes from a poor family background. Maggi lost his father when he was eight years old. His mother had to raise her seven children on her own in a suburb of Zurich. Maggi was often hungry.
- **his occupations:** Maggi was trained as gardener but has always liked to cook. Later, he made his hobby his profession and worked as a chef. Since 1984 he has spent his free time guerilla gardening.
- **his intentions:** Maggi wants to preserve plants that are in danger of becoming extinct, likes to add unusual ingredients to his meals and would like to provide free herbs for everybody.
- **how Maggi's guerilla activities are received:** Maggi and some pupils have sown edible plants in an area employing traffic calming measures; the city of Zurich has not uprooted any spots in which guerilla gardeners have sown seeds.

b) *Sample solution:*

The newspaper article „Mit beiden Beinen im Salat" written by Jessica Braun and published in the German weekly *Die ZEIT,* is about 58-year-old Maurice Maggi, the oldest guerilla gardener in Zurich. Maggi, who was trained as a gardener, but always liked cooking, eventually turned his hobby into a job and worked as a chef. Since 1984 he has been planting seeds in public parks and even a churchyard. Whenever he needs fresh ingredients to give the meals he prepares a special flavour, Maggi goes out and collects wild herbs for free. He knows where it is safe to pick the edible plants and has even involved pupils in planting wild herbs.

Maggi's intention as a guerilla gardener is to preserve endangered herbs and, at the same time, make them available to everybody at no extra cost. He comes from a poor family background and knows that in economically hard times many people have problems making ends meet and welcome free herbs for cooking. With the tacit approval of the city council, Maurice Maggi and some pupils have planted seeds of rare herbs in flower boxes in an area employing traffic calming measures. *(192 words)*

Ich hab's gemacht

46 a) ll. 1–25: Teenager William Kamkwamba from Malawi becomes famous
ll. 26–38: William Kamkwamba's construction of a wind turbine
ll. 39–49: William Kamkwamba's further education

b) *Sample solution:*

The boy who could not wait for miracles

The world learnt about William Kamkwamba, an African teenager from Malawi, when a blogger wrote on his website about how William had built a wind turbine from scrap material all by himself. A video that showed William being interviewed by scientists at the TED conference, an annual meeting focusing on developments in technology, entertainment and design, was put on the Internet and attracted worldwide attention. Aged 14, William, who comes from a very poor family, had to leave school because his parents could no longer afford the fees. Out of curiosity, the boy picked up a book in the village library on how wind turbines can be used to generate electricity. William decided to build one out of an old bicycle and material he had collected from the local scrapyard. Many of his fellow villagers did not believe in him, but William finally succeeded and his wind turbine produced enough electricity to light his family home.

Boston Consulting immediately recognised William Kamkwamba's potential and, amongst other sponsors, agreed to provide a scholarship of $ 20,000 to enable William to attend a private college and prepare for his A-levels. We are very pleased to invest in education to help talented young Africans make their way to university. University graduates are expected to work in Africa for at least ten years and can thus contribute their share to improve the state and future of the continent. And we have not been disappointed by William Kamkwamba: Having sat his A-levels at the "African Leadership Academy", in Johannesburg, he moved on to study at Dartmouth College in New Hampshire, from which he has meanwhile graduated. His amazing achievements make us proud and underline our mission.

(281 words)

Überleben üben in den Everglades

47 a)

Advantages of a prepper's life	Disadvantages of a prepper's life
• cheap, basic lifestyle (food, clothes) • living in harmony with nature • environmentally friendly tourism • experience of self-reliance and independence • preparation for emergencies	• uncomfortable lifestyle (e.g. hygiene) • time-consuming way of life • survival skills required • lack of amenities (no Internet, no smartphone) • mosquitos

b) *Sample solution:*

Hi Amanda,

I'm really looking forward to spending my summer holidays with you in Florida. What a brilliant idea to go on a prepping course for a couple of days! At first, I didn't really know what prepping was all about, but then I searched the Internet and I think it would be an interesting experience for the two of us. I realise that it can be a bit uncomfortable at times sleeping rough and eating all sorts of plants or perhaps even beetles! Lighting a fire from scratch without any matches will also be a challenge, I imagine.

However, on the other hand, it would be great to learn a few new skills which may be useful some time, you never know. I wonder how I will cope without my smart phone. That will be the real survival test for me. Anyway, thanks for suggesting such an adventure!

As to the rest of our time in the Everglades, I would prefer to go camping, if that's ok with you. The hotels seem rather expensive, and I think sleeping in a tent is much more fun. The Flamingo Campground might be a good idea. Could you check if they still have free camping spots? By the time we arrive at the campground, we will know how to prepare a tasty meal from grass and herbs …

Please let me know if I need to bring any special equipment for the prep course and forward the reply of the campground to me as well. Bye for now and lots of love to you and the family. I can hardly wait till August!

Emily *(272 words)*

Das Ende des Konsumwahns: Leben zum Nulltarif?

48 a)

	Statement	Order
A	The new legislation applies to all larger supermarkets.	7
B	Many people are afraid to eat food that is past its best-before date.	4
C	A lot of food is thrown away although it is perfectly edible.	2
D	In France, edible surplus food has to be given to charity or must be reused as animal food or in farming.	6
E	Organisations like Foodsaver collect food that is not wanted anymore.	3
F	It is the aim of the government to cut the wastage of food by half.	8
G	Leading a life like Marius's creates many challenges in everyday life.	5
H	However, with their 5 per cent share, supermarkets are responsible for only a tiny amount of the food that is thrown away every year.	9
I	Refusing to consume is a way of protesting against mass consumption and a senseless waste of resources.	1

b) *Sample solution:*

Have you ever bought something in a shop which you later realised you already had? Have you ever brought home too many yoghurts and too much fresh fruit which you then forgot about and had to throw away because the apples didn't look appetising anymore, and the yoghurt had passed its best-before date? Well, sadly, it happens to all of us. Our materialistic society works on consumption, you might argue.

However, there are brave people who say "Stop!" Marius Diab, a student living in Munich, even goes as far as to avoid spending any money at all. He eats, sleeps and travels for free, only paying his health insurance and university fees. Feeding himself is no problem at all, he says, because supermarkets, shops and restaurants waste enormous amounts of food. In view of the large numbers of poor and disadvantaged people in our society, this is a disgrace. Politicians in France have meanwhile taken action: A new law forbids supermarkets to throw away food which is still fit for consumption. Instead, it must be given to poor people or be used as animal feed or in farming. Unfortunately, this only applies to larger supermarkets.

I think this is a good idea and would like Germany to follow the French example. But apart from this, everyone can do something to prevent the wastage in general – this would have a bigger impact on society than regulations can have. Start thinking twice about your own consumption habits.

Do you really need what you just bought? Remember the old saying: Waste not, want not! There is so much truth in that – especially in our materialistic society. *(275 words)*

Kenn dein Limit vs. Schockbilder für Raucher

49 a) The idea behind plain packaging is to generate a layout that is as simple as possible to make products of different brands look identical and less competitive. In this case, Ireland is the first country in the EU to make plain packaging for all cigarette brands obligatory. There is no individual colour scheme and the brand name has to be written in small letters and in a plain style only. Additionally, shocking pictures and warning labels are intended to inform smokers about the consequences their addiction might have for their health.

b)

Advantages of plain packaging	Disadvantages of plain packaging
• no opportunity for tobacco industry to use packaging for advertising • loss of attraction to teenagers and children (as products no longer work as a status symbol)	• promotion of price wars, smuggling and product piracy • interference with property rights of tobacco companies

c) The poster, which shows two girls in two completely different situations, warns young people of excessive drinking. In the larger part of the picture, you can see a girl who seems to be completely drunk and who is no longer able to stand up. Together with a paramedic, her friend helps her to get onto a stretcher. The whole scene might be taking place in front of a night club, as the girl is dressed in a party outfit, wearing a tight top and short skirt. The girl might have to be taken to hospital with alcohol poisoning. In the smaller picture, which is placed in the middle of the larger picture and looks like a Polaroid photo, you can see the two girls having fun. Both look quite sober and are smiling happily at each other. They give the impression of being best friends. “Know your limit”, the caption urges, in order to “share everything” (the fun, in this case) and not to “lose a lot” (such as health, friendship, dignity and self-respect).

d) *Sample solution:*

Every day 15,000 people all over the world die of smoking-related diseases, which illustrates the enormous health hazard of smoking. Alcohol abuse, especially underage drinking, is just as dangerous. What can be done to increase awareness – especially among young people? Many countries have meanwhile introduced a ban on smoking in public places and in restaurants. Germany raised taxes on "alcopops", sweet alcoholic drinks that had been popular, especially amongst teenagers. Both measures had a positive impact.

Recently, Ireland passed a law demanding tobacco companies sell cigarettes in plain packaging in order to destroy the appeal packaging might have on teenagers in particular. To combat the problem of teenage drinking, the health authorities in Germany launched a campaign warning young adults about the harmful consequences of alcohol abuse with posters and photos illustrating what might happen if you drink too much.

Evaluating these two strategies – posters and plain packaging – I would say that obligatory plain packaging is a rather drastic measure, but I believe it will yield positive results. Adolescents especially, who often take up smoking because of peer pressure, will be shocked by the graphic images. As one of the last opportunities for advertising will be done away with, fewer teenagers might be attracted to cigarettes altogether. However, I don't believe that the anti-drinking campaign will be as effective, as people can just look the other way. Instead, alcohol must be made even more expensive to put drinks out of the reach of many teens. Posters alone won't get the message across.

Thank you for your attention. *(257 words)*

Fighting obesity

50 a) • **Was ist das Problem?**

- Fettleibigkeit und generell schlechter Ernährungszustand
- hohe Zahl fettleibiger und schlecht ernährter Kinder und Jugendlicher in Großbritannien
- 70 000 Todesfälle jährlich aufgrund ungesunder Ernährung in Großbritannien
- 24 000 Menschen sterben jährlich an den Folgen von übermäßigem Softdrink-Genuss in Mexiko (vgl. Statistik)

- Befürchtung eines Anstiegs der Zahl zuckerkranker Menschen
- enorme finanzielle Belastung des Gesundheitssystems

- **Welche Gründe bzw. Ursachen werden für das Problem genannt?**
  - hoher Konsum von überzuckerten Getränken und Fast Food
  - geringer Konsum von Obst und Gemüse, da zu teuer für Geringverdiener
- **Was kann getan werden?**
  - höhere Steuern auf ungesunde Nahrungsmittel und Getränke für Kinder
  - gesetzliche Verpflichtung, ein bestimmtes Mindestmaß an gesundem Essen in den Schulkantinen anzubieten
  - Verbot, mehrere Fast-Food-Ketten in unmittelbarer Nähe zueinander zu bauen
  - Subventionierung von Obst und Gemüse
  - freiwillige Selbstverpflichtung der Nahrungsmittelindustrie, den Zuckergehalt in Lebensmitteln zu senken

b) *Sample solution:*

Fit statt fett – Bring dich in Form!

Alarmierende Nachrichten kommen aus Großbritannien: 70 000 Menschen sterben jährlich, weil sie schlecht ernährt sind. Die Ärzte beklagen, dass die Briten zu wenig vitaminreiche Kost, wie z. B. Obst und Gemüse, essen und stattdessen in Mengen Fast Food und gezuckerte Softdrinks zu sich nehmen. Die Folgen sind ein allgemein schlechter Ernährungszustand, Fettleibigkeit und Diabetes. Daher schlagen Gesundheitsexperten Alarm und rufen nach drastischen Maßnahmen: Es soll eine Zuckersteuer geben, wenn die Hersteller der Getränke den Zuckergehalt ihrer Produkte nicht verringern. Zudem wird gefordert, Obst und Gemüse zu subventionieren, damit es für alle erschwinglich wird. In Mexiko, wo besonders viele Menschen wegen übermäßigen Genusses von Softdrinks sterben, zeigt eine zehnprozentige Zusatzsteuer erste positive Auswirkungen. Aber man muss nicht nach Mexiko gehen, um die katastrophalen Folgen schlechter Ernährung zu beobachten. Auch in Deutschland sind zu viele zuckerhaltige Getränke die Todesursache von Tausenden Erwachsenen.

Wie sieht deine Ernährung aus? Treibst du regelmäßig Sport oder läufst du Gefahr, dich zum Couch-Potato zu entwickeln? Lass es nicht so weit kommen! Trainier dich fit, mach den Computer aus, leg das Smartphone weg und sorge für Bewegung. Dazu brauchst du nicht in ein teures Fitness-Studio zu gehen. Auf unserer Homepage www.jung-und-fit.de kannst du dir das PDF „Fit fürs Leben“ mit vielen Tipps für ein gesundes Leben kostenlos downloaden. Lass nicht erst die Politiker mit einem Gesetz über dein Wohlbefinden entscheiden, tu selber was. Übernimm die Verantwortung für deine Gesundheit – am besten zusammen mit anderen, dann macht Fitness noch mehr Spaß. *(250 Wörter)*

Tattoo removal is big business

51 a)

	Vorteile	Nachteile
Laser-technologie	• Korrekturen an der Oberfläche der Haut	• langwierig und teuer • keine Garantie für vollständige Entfernung • ungeeignet für dunklere Haut
Injektion einer Flüssigkeit	• preisgünstiger als Laser	• nicht geeignet für alte, tief unter die Haut gehende und großflächige Tattoos
Chirurgischer Eingriff	• schmerzlos • vollständige Entfernung des Tattoos	• ähnlich teuer wie Lasertechnologie • langwierig • nicht geeignet für große Tattoos (z. B. Ärmel) und straffe Hautpartien

b) *Sample solution:*

Hallo Lara,

ich habe von Mia gehört, dass du dir dein Tattoo entfernen lassen willst. Zufällig habe ich im Englischunterricht einen Artikel über das Thema gelesen und dachte, er könnte dich interessieren. Ganz billig wird es leider nicht werden, aber es gibt immerhin verschiedene Möglichkeiten.

Mit Laserstrahlen kann man zum Beispiel die Farbe des Tattoos auflösen, die Farbpartikel gelangen dann ins Blut und werden vom Körper abgebaut. Das ist allerdings teuer und man braucht wahrscheinlich mehrere Sitzungen. Leider gibt es auch keine Garantie, dass die Tätowierung damit ganz verschwindet.

Dann gibt es eine Methode, bei der eine spezielle Flüssigkeit unter die tätowierte Haut gespritzt wird. Ähnlich wie bei der Laserbehandlung wird die Farbe in kleine Einzelbestandteile aufgespalten und vom Körper abgebaut. Das ist billiger als die Laser-Variante, eignet sich aber nicht für ältere und großflächige Tattoos.
Wenn du mit Sicherheit dein Tattoo loswerden möchtest, bietet sich der chirurgische Eingriff an, der ungefähr so viel kostet wie die Laserbehandlung. Die Operation verläuft schmerzlos, weil sie unter Narkose durchgeführt wird. Große Tätowierungen lassen sich damit aber leider nicht entfernen und an Stellen, an denen die Haut sehr straff gespannt ist (z. B. Ellbogen und Knie), kommt die Methode wohl auch nicht infrage.
Ich hoffe, dass ich dir weiterhelfen konnte und dass du die richtige Entscheidung treffen wirst. Lass gerne von dir hören.

Viele Grüße
Moritz *(223 Wörter)*

The generation gap

52 a) Junge Briten zwischen 20 und 30 Jahren dürfen nicht hoffen, denselben hohen **Lebensstandard** zu erreichen wie ihre Eltern und Großeltern. Nach Abschluss ihres Studiums stehen junge Erwachsene oft vor erheblichen Problemen. Aufgrund hoher **Studiengebühren** in Großbritannien haben sie einen Berg **Schulden** und oft ist es Ihnen nicht möglich, eine **Anstellung/Beschäftigung** zu finden, die ihrer **Ausbildung/Qualifikation** entspricht. In schlecht bezahlten Jobs ist aber der **Verdienst** häufig nicht hoch genug, um sich eine eigene **Wohnung** oder gar die Gründung einer **Familie** leisten zu können. Zu all diesen Belastungen kommt aber noch die Tatsache, dass junge Menschen für die **Versorgung** der Rentner und Pensionäre aufkommen müssen.
Allein die Rente der Babyboomer-Generation liegt oft deutlich über dem **Durchschnittseinkommen** vieler Arbeitnehmer. Auch werden Rentnern oft **Vergünstigungen** wie verbilligte **Fahrkarten** im öffentlichen Nahverkehr und Steuerentlastungen angeboten. Durch die Wohnungsknappheit gewinnen zudem ihre **Immobilien** an Wert, was aber auch dazu führt, dass junge Menschen sie sich nicht leisten können.
Aus Angst vor dem Verlust von **Wählerstimmen** verschließen **Politiker** die Augen vor dieser Entwicklung. Dabei wären auch viele ältere Wähler bereit, für die Zukunft ihrer Kinder und Enkel **Einschnitte** zu akzeptieren,

um die finanzielle Lage des Landes zu **verbessern**, wenn es ein vernünftiges **Konzept** zur Verteilung der **Belastungen** auf alle Generationen gibt.

b) *Sample solution:*

Sehr geehrte Frau Dr. Raismann-Koch,

in Bezug auf Generationengerechtigkeit liefert Großbritannien ein abschreckendes Beispiel. Die Situation der jüngeren Generation ist dort bedeutend schlechter als die ihrer Eltern und Großeltern. Viele junge Briten sind aufgrund von Studiengebühren hoch verschuldet. Beim Eintritt in das Berufsleben finden nur wenige Absolventen eine ihrer Ausbildung entsprechende Arbeit und müssen sich mit anspruchslosen und schlechter bezahlten Anstellungen zufriedengeben. Wer kein eigenes Geld verdient, kann nicht selbstständig werden und ist oft gezwungen, auch mit Mitte bzw. Ende zwanzig noch bei seinen Eltern zu wohnen. Wie soll man unter diesen Umständen eine Familie gründen? Leider sieht es derzeit auch in Deutschland eher schlecht aus: Man spricht von der „Generation Praktikum“: Monatelang werden Berufseinsteiger ohne Bezahlung beschäftigt und dann nicht eingestellt.
In einem Artikel des *Daily Telegraph* äußert die britische Journalistin Katie Morley den Verdacht, dass vonseiten der Politik gar kein Interesse besteht, die Situation zu verbessern, da man Angst hat, sich den Unmut der Rentner und Pensionäre zuzuziehen, die derzeit – sowohl in Deutschland als auch in Großbritannien – eine erhebliche Wählergruppe stellen. Sie fordert Politiker auf, ein Wahlprogramm zu verfassen, in dem eine fairere Verteilung der finanziellen Lasten auf alle Generationen dargelegt wird.
Auch in Deutschland wäre eine Debatte und eine anschließende Beschlussfassung zum Thema Generationengerechtigkeit dringend notwendig, um der jungen Generation bessere Startmöglichkeiten zu bieten, d. h. insbesondere faire Bezahlung für Berufsanfänger und eine verstärkte Förderung junger Familien, damit Beruf und Familie besser vereinbar sind. Bitte setzen Sie sich dafür ein, dass alle Praktikanten wenigstens den Mindestlohn erhalten, um so eine Existenzgrundlage für Menschen in prekären Arbeitsverhältnissen zu schaffen.

Mit freundlichen Grüßen
Anna-Lena Bergmann *(265 Wörter)*

Language in Use: Grammar

Adjectives and adverbs

53 The **most recent** discovery of human bone fragments in Africa is a scientific sensation. The bones which were discovered in Ethiopia are 500,000 years **older** than any human remains found before. These fossils represent our **oldest** direct human ancestors. With these bones scientists will be able to carry out the **most detailed** investigation into the origins of man and ideas about how our ancestors lived. The **most fascinating** aspect of the discovery are the 20 teeth which were excavated. The findings suggest that those humans were **most likely** vegetarians. Remains of plants and seeds were found **more frequently** with the skeletons than bones of animals. That is why it is **more likely** that they ate plants and fruit than that they hunted animals. They **most certainly** made no stone tools.

54 Shirley Binghall works as a conservator in the British Museum. Her job is to keep the **valuable** objects in **good** condition so that they look **beautiful** when they are displayed **publicly**. Because of her **extremely long** experience Shirley knows **exactly** how to look after the artefacts **properly**. Last week she was given an **exceptionally difficult** job. German archaeologists in Troy had **carefully** unearthed **numerous** pieces of a pot that was **probably** Greek. Although the dirty-brown pieces looked **fairly worthless** at first sight, Shirley knew **immediately** that the Germans had found a **real** beauty. Shirley **carefully** placed all the pieces on her working table. There they look **just** like a jigsaw puzzle. Then Shirley **cautiously** cleaned the pieces and tried to fit them together. For several days she worked **regularly** on repairing the object. Using sellotape, plaster and wax, Shirley **finally** succeeded in sticking the pieces into place. Although several pieces were missing, she didn't find it **hard** to date the pot **correctly**. She **hardly** ever tries to paint over the missing pieces, in order to give the visitors a **clear** picture of which parts are old and which have **recently** been added.

The tenses

55 a) Hey Jeff, **have you ever been** to Scotland?
b) Yes, I **went** there last year with my parents.
c) While you **were driving** along the lake, **did you observe** anything mysterious?
d) No, I **didn't see** the monster then if that's what you mean. But when we **went** into the museum I **looked at** a giant-size model of Nessie.
e) For more than sixty years people **have claimed** that they **have seen** "Nessie". In 1934 one even **said** he had taken a picture! But now, it **has just been proved** that the photo was a fake.
f) I **have never believed** in that legend anyway!

56 Hotel directors, castle owners and tourist managers **are always trying** to think of new ways of attracting more guests and visitors. Many **have even played** with the idea of inventing a spectacular ghost or monster, such as Nessie. The legendary creature which is supposed **to be living** in Loch Ness **still arouses** the interest of tourists. For decades Nessie **has been drawing** large numbers of visitors to the lonely lake in the Scottish Highlands.
The Argentinian version of Nessie **is called** Nahuelito. Local Indians maintain that a monster **has been living** in the Nahuel Huapi Lake since ancient times. The lake, which **covers** 318 square miles, **lies** at the foot of the Patagonian mountains. At present, plans **are being discussed** to build a visitor centre. Scores of tourists are convinced that they have seen a huge snake-like creature in the water while they **were driving** along the shores of the lake. In bars and restaurants in Bariloche you can listen to visitors who **are telling** stories about their sightings. One of them said he **was sitting** on the edge of the lake fishing when suddenly a hump **appeared** from under the surface. In spite of reports like this one, there are still many people who **do not believe** in monsters or ghosts.

57 About five years ago I **travelled** to Scotland for the first time and **was fascinated** immediately by the beautiful landscape, the romantic castles and the historic sites. It **rained** almost every day when I **explored/was exploring** the Highlands, but that **did not worry** me as friends who **had been** to Scotland before **warned/had warned** me. I **wasn't/had not been able** to go hiking on my first trip so I **decided** to come back as soon as possible. Two years later, I **persuaded** my friends Simon and Marc to accompany me on a rambling tour through the Grampians. Both **love** the Highlands because they **(had) visited** Scotland when they **were** teenagers but **have not been** back since. Early summer **is** a good season for hiking, so Marc, Simon and I **will/are going to set out** on another trip to Scotland next June. We **must save/will have to save** a lot of money to buy our camping equipment. We **will buy** our flight tickets soon because I'm afraid prices **will go** up again before the summer season starts. I'm sure we **will enjoy** our tour and that this **will not be** my last visit to that beautiful country.

58
a) The bread fruit trees are used as a cheap source of food by the plantation owners.
b) He will be asked to join by all his friends.
c) The older man was respected for his abilities as a seaman by Fletcher.
d) The son is being taught how to draw a chart by the old sailor.
e) Orders were not obeyed by the lazy sailors.
f) The ship had been burnt by the mutineers.
g) Bligh's voyage is regarded as a masterpiece in navigation (by us).
h) Seven of his 18 men were lost.
i) In 1817 he was buried in London.
j) The story has been used for a novel by two American writers.
k) A profit is still being made with the film on the mutiny by the MGM film company.

59
a) The Egyptian embalmers took out all the organs and preserved them separately.
b) They only left the heart in place.
c) They drew the brain out of the head through the nose.
d) The Egyptian embalmers cleaned the body and filled it with spices and herbs.
e) They used bags of white powder, natron, to dry the body.
f) Finally they wrapped it in many layers of linen bandages.
g) The Egyptian embalmers put a mask over the face.
h) Then they put the body into a coffin.
i) The Egyptian embalmers used several coffins to protect the mummy.

Relative clauses

60 In November 2013, Prince Harry joined one of three teams **whose** aim it was to trek more than 200 miles to the South Pole. The teams consisted of servicemen and -women from the UK and other nations, **who** had suffered terrible war injuries. The prince, **who** was patron of the expedition, belonged to Team UK, **which** included four injured British soldiers. Due to the extreme weather conditions the expedition teams were followed by a support team, **who/which** were on hand in case of emergencies. The adventure, **which** lasted for more than three weeks, was successfully completed on December 13, 2013. Ed Parker, the director **who** led the expedition, said, "We always knew that this wasn't going to be easy, but we were determined to get 12 men and women, all injured in conflict, to the South Pole".

Reaching the South Pole was not the only purpose (**that**) the organisers had in mind; in fact, what was more important was to raise money for military charities. Harry, **who** after his father, his brother and the latter's children is next in line to the throne, is the first member of the Royal Family to trek to the geographic South Pole. In the past, he had sometimes been the subject of reports **which** wanted to show him as a careless party-goer. However, the prince has dedicated a lot of his time working for a good cause. The expedition to the South Pole was not the first charity work (**that**) Harry has taken part in. He was a member of the charity's trek **which** headed to the North Pole in 2011. **What** kept him from completing the expedition then was his brother's wedding, **which** he had to attend.

61
a) There is a triangle in the Atlantic Ocean, one corner of which is the island of Bermuda.
b) The Bermuda Triangle is a vast stretch of open sea which covers more than 1 million square miles. / The Bermuda Triangle, which covers more than 1 million square miles, is a vast stretch of open sea.
c) In 1945 the crews of five torpedo bombers, who had been on a training flight, were lost over the Bermuda Triangle.
d) In September 1950 an article was published in the *Miami Herald* which reported the unusual disappearances of several ships and planes.
e) Over the years more planes and ships whose disappearance could not be explained made the headlines.
f) Numerous theories, none of which is convincing, have been put forward about the mysterious disappearances.

g) Hollywood producers who were sure that the subject would interest people made several films and TV series about the Bermuda Triangle.

62 a) I will never forget the film *Avatar*, **which** I saw when I was twelve.
b) The science fiction film tells a story **(which is)** set on a planet in the distant future.
c) The action takes place on the moon Pandora, **whose** atmosphere is poisonous to humans.
d) Pandora is inhabited by blue-skinned humanoids **who/that** live in harmony with nature.
e) The director of the film was James Cameron, **who** had made the box-office hit *Titanic*.
f) The money **(which/that)** Cameron had earned with *Titanic* was invested in the development of *Avatar*.
g) *Avatar* made use of actors **who/that** had been generated by computers.
h) It contains everything **(that)** cinema-goers could wish for.
i) The movie, **which** won three Oscars, became the most profitable film of all time.

Conditional clauses

63 a) If there **weren't/wasn't** any gravity, things would float around in the air.
b) Things **wouldn't fall** to the ground if there wasn't any gravity.
c) Astronauts **couldn't survive** in space if they didn't wear space suits.
d) Astronauts couldn't have walked on the moon if they **hadn't worn** space suits.
e) If we travelled at the speed of light, we **could visit** other planets.
f) We could visit other planets if they **weren't** so far away.
g) If the astronauts didn't do any exercise during their flights, their muscles **would get** weak because of weightlessness.
h) If satellites **didn't have** solar panels, they wouldn't have any energy for their instruments.
i) Weather forecasts **would have been** more precise years ago if meteorologists had had weather satellites earlier.
j) If there weren't any TV satellites in space, live broadcasts from other continents **wouldn't be** possible.
k) TV satellites wouldn't stay above the same place all the time if they **didn't move** in time with the Earth.

64 a) If everything goes according to plan, the Space Agency ...

- [ ] presented a number of spectacular space projects soon.
- [ ] would present a number of spectacular space projects soon.
- [x] will present a number of spectacular space projects soon.

b) A robot to Mars could be launched soon if funds ...

- [ ] were available in time.
- [x] are available in time.
- [ ] will be available in time.

c) Sending probes into space would be cheaper if weight ...

- [ ] isn't such a big problem.
- [x] wasn't such a big problem.
- [ ] would not be such a big problem.

d) If engineers knew more about suitable landing sites, spacecrafts ...

- [x] could be landed more safely.
- [ ] would have been landed more safely.
- [ ] would have landed more safely.

e) If the solar panels had unfolded properly, the robot ...

- [ ] could drill into the Martian soil for a longer period.
- [x] could have drilled into the Martian soil for a longer period.
- [ ] can drill into the Martian soil for a longer period.

f) The government would supply more funds if the general public ...

- [ ] supports space exploration more enthusiastically.
- [x] supported space exploration more enthusiastically.
- [ ] will support space exploration more enthusiastically.

g) If NASA had not been so successful in the past, funds ...

- [x] would have been cut.
- [ ] will be cut.
- [ ] were cut.

h) If science fiction authors were right, time travel …
- [ ] is easy.
- [x] would be easy.
- [ ] could have been possible.

i) If mission control loses contact, the robot …
- [ ] would not have been able to explore more sites.
- [ ] would not be able to explore more sites.
- [x] will not be able to explore more sites.

Modal auxiliaries

65 He **must be regarded** as a typical example of the video game generation. When he was young Daniel just **could not get** enough of ghost stories and fairy tales about gnomes and wizards. His mother **didn't have to call** him twice when it was time for a bedtime story. No wonder Daniel **could hardly wait** until he was bought his first computer and computer games. Although he **was only allowed to play** after he had finished his homework, his mother often **had to remind** him to stop gaming and go out for a change. On Saturdays Daniel **could not play**, because he worked in a supermarket to earn extra pocket money so that he **could afford** to buy more games. He **didn't have to spend/didn't need to spend** too much as he **was able to share/could share** costs with his friend Jason, another online game addict. Sometimes they joined a LAN party, where they **could play/were able to play** for hours. Last month Daniel took his final exams, in which he **could have done** better if he hadn't spent so much time on his computer. You **needn't tell/don't have to tell** him that, though – he knows it himself. After the holidays he **will have to stop** playing video and online games for hours on end, as he **will have to start** preparing for university, which starts in October. His younger brother Harry often asks him whether he **will be allowed to play** on Daniel's computer then.

66 A) I won't have to book my holiday tomorrow.

B) You don't have to/need not/needn't clean the whole plate.

C) We don't have to change clothes.

D) I didn't have to wait (ages) at the bus stop (as he showed up on time).

E) For hot meals, you don't have to/need not/needn't pay in advance.

F) You don't have to/needn't be home before ten.

Reported speech

67 a) Old Spencer wanted to know why my marks were getting worse.
b) Old Spencer asked if I had any problems at home.
c) He inquired whether I didn't want to go to school anymore.
d) Old Spencer wanted to know when I went to bed at night.
e) Old Spencer asked what time I did my homework.
f) He inquired whether a parent was there when I get home from school.
g) Old Spencer wanted to know if I saw my father every day.
h) He asked if I had any financial worries.

68 a) He advised me to think about what was more important: pocket money or school.
b) He told me to tell my parents about my job.
c) He told me not to work too many hours.
d) He advised me not to do any hard manual work.
e) He told me to avoid working before I had a test at school.
f) He advised me to work on Saturdays only.
g) He told me to avoid working late at night.
h) He advised me not to do any shift work.

The gerund and the participles

69 a) Ed admitted **having seen** the film before, so he didn't really feel like **watching** it again.
b) Tom, however, said, "I think that film is well worth **seeing** twice."
c) But Ed wasn't convinced: "Who would want **to go** and see a film for the second time!?"
d) Anne interrupted before Tom could answer: "And what about me? Has anybody asked me what I would like **to do** tonight?"
e) Ed: "Well, what about you then? Would you prefer **to go** to the cinema, to a disco or to a restaurant?"

f) Anne: "I don't fancy **sitting** in a dark cinema for three hours. And I can't imagine the two of you **dancing** with me in the 'The Millenium Club'! So let's go to MacBeef's!"
g) Tom: "I detest **eating** fast food that tastes of nothing!"
h) Ed: "If you don't enjoy **eating** out, why don't you stay at home!"
i) Finally Anne said, "Oh, stop **arguing**. Let's go and see the film, have a snack and go to the disco afterwards."

70 a) I think many young people would **enjoy playing** in a pop group.
b) One day my friends Jeff and Morris suggested forming a pop group because we **are interested in making** music.
c) They thought **we would have no difficulty (in) playing** a couple of numbers together.
d) We didn't really know what songs to choose, but one night Jeff suggested, "**How about picking** some golden oldies that everybody likes?"
e) In the end, we **succeeded in rehearsing** some old Stones numbers.
f) We **look/We're looking forward to playing** at our youth club next Friday.

71 a) An international convention **held** in New York banned the sale of ivory.
b) Tourists **interested** in watching herds of elephants were pleased about the news.
c) **Depending on** tourism, many African countries profited from the ban.
d) **Supporting** the move in general, international organisations like Greenpeace also pointed out some problems **arising** from the ban.
e) **Increasing** the number of protected regions, the countries attracted more tourists.
f) The arrival of larger numbers of tourists spoiled parts of the areas **meant** to be protected.

72 a) The campaign for the protection of apes and rhinos **which was started** by US and Japanese scientists attracted the interest of the world public.
b) Cameramen made TV films **which showed** the cruelties of poachers in the national parks.
c) **After they had seen** the pictures, TV viewers wrote letters of protest.
d) The civil war **which took place** in Rwanda almost destroyed one of the last habitats of African mountain gorillas.

e) **As they did not have** enough land to grow food, the farmers invaded Rwanda's Volcanoes National Park.
f) The rebels **who seized** control of the park were Tutsis, an ethnic group **which tried** to get back land **which they/it had lost/which had been lost** more than three decades ago.
g) They destroyed a research centre **which had been run** for nearly two decades by the American naturalist Dian Fossey whose pioneering work with the great apes was made famous by the film *Gorillas in the Mist.*

Language in Use: Vocabulary

Test your vocabulary knowledge

73 The 19th **century** – the Victorian Age – was a time of great prosperity in England. The population **increased** tremendously: in 1811 England had 12 million inhabitants, by 1851 that number had risen to 21 million. The Industrial Revolution and the growth of the Empire made factory owners and merchants rich. Under the golden surface there was a lower class whose life was characterised by poverty, **misery** and crime. Thousands of workers left the countryside in **search** of jobs in the towns. What they found were low **wages** and badly built houses. The little money they earned was not enough to support themselves and their families. If they could not pay their **debts**, they had to go to **prison**. Gradually, more and more **educated** people became aware of the great **injustices** and the social problems of the age and tried to **introduce** reforms. An important member of that reform movement was one of the greatest writers of English literature: Charles Dickens. In his very popular novels Dickens described the **dreadful** conditions in which poor people had to live. He wanted to make his readers **aware** that social reforms were necessary to improve the lives of the **underprivileged** masses. Dickens knew very well what he was writing about because in his early childhood he had **experienced** what it meant to be poor.

74 Alexander Selkirk was the son of a shoemaker born in Largo in the Fife region in Scotland. As a young boy, he was hard to control and got into trouble with almost everyone. After **arguing** with **many** of **his** neighbours, **he** left **home** and **ran** away **to** sea. Selkirk **was** 19 **years** of **age** then.
In 1703 he **became** a **sailor** on a **pirate** ship, but **could** not **stand** the **discipline** on **board**. After **an** argument **with** the **captain**, he **asked** to **be** put **ashore** on **the** nearest **island**. He **wanted** to **live** on **his** own. The **ship** was **near** the Juan Fernández **Island(s)**, off **the** coast **of** Chile. In **October** 1704 Selkirk **was** left **behind** on an **uninhabited** island, a **beautiful** place **with** rich **vegetation**. There **were** plenty **of** goats **which** Selkirk **could** hunt. There **were** no **people** at **all** and Selkirk **enjoyed** the **silence**. After **more** than 4 **years** of **being** alone, **he** decided **that** he **had** had **enough**. In 1709, he **saw** two **ships** off **the** coast and **lit** a **fire** to **attract** their **attention**. One **of** the **ships** sent a **boat** ashore **to** pick **up** Alexander Selkirk. It **took** him **back** to **civilisation** again. He **died** in 1721.

The **English** writer Daniel Defoe **heard** of Selkirk's **story** and **wrote** a **novel** based **on** Selkirk's **experience**. He called it *The Life and Strange Surprising Adventures of Robinson Crusoe.*

75 A) search B) convoy C) expedition D) refuge E) proposal F) supply G) trace H) discover

76 For centuries the impressive **location** of the castle has **fascinated** visitors from all over the country. It is **situated** high on a hill on the rough **coast** of Cornwall near the little village of Tintagel: People call it "King Arthur's castle". However, when you have climbed the steep **path** to the top there is not much to see today: a number of low **stone** walls which might be the **remains** of a hall, of a well and perhaps a few graves. What is more breathtaking is the fantastic **view** of the rocks and the sea – and the thought of a legendary **connection** between the castle and King Arthur. Could this be the place where Arthur was **born**, where Merlin, the magician, hid the baby from his **enemies**? "Merlin's Cave" is the name of a rock formation down by the **waves** that you can see from the top of the castle. Is this the place where King Arthur and his Knights of the Round Table held their **meetings**? At least this is what the villagers of Tintagel and the local tourist **board** would have you believe.

It all **began** in the 12th century, when Geoffrey of Monmouth **recorded** the legend of King Arthur in his *History of the Kings of Britain.* He made Tintagel the scene where it all **happened**. Many writers **followed** who took up the story of Arthur and his great court at Camelot, among them Alfred Lord Tennyson (1809–1892). **Between** 1859 and 1888 he completed *Idylls of the King*, an Arthurian epic in 12 **parts**. All romantic writers of the nineteenth century kept **alive** the traditional **connection** with Tintagel Castle, not knowing what had **really** happened in the past. There was no **scientific** proof, as **archaeology** was still in its infancy. However, the stories became extremely **popular**, and the link between Arthur and Tintagel was **stronger** than ever.

Archaeologists began **excavations** at Tintagel in 1933. They found out that the **ruins** we see today are the remains of a Norman **castle** built in the 12th century. The **question**, though, is why did Reginald, Earl of Cornwall, build a castle at a **place** which is of little strategic **value**? Moreover, the castle could not have been an **important** one because it was only used for a relatively **short** time. People lived in it for only a **hundred** years or so and by the fourteenth century it had **fallen** into disrepair. Later it was used as a **prison**. So, that medieval castle could not have been Arthur's castle after all! If Arthur were not just a legendary **figure**, he would have lived in the sixth century, well before Tintagel was **built**. Consequently, the link that Geoffrey had made was the result of **complete** fantasy.

77

MENIAL	HIRE	ILLITERATE
ABUSE	EMPLOY	DISREGARD
INJURY	PERMIT	RESTRICTION
EARN	COMPLAIN	UNSKILLED
LABOUR	FACTORY	EXPLOITATION
FILTHY	POVERTY	

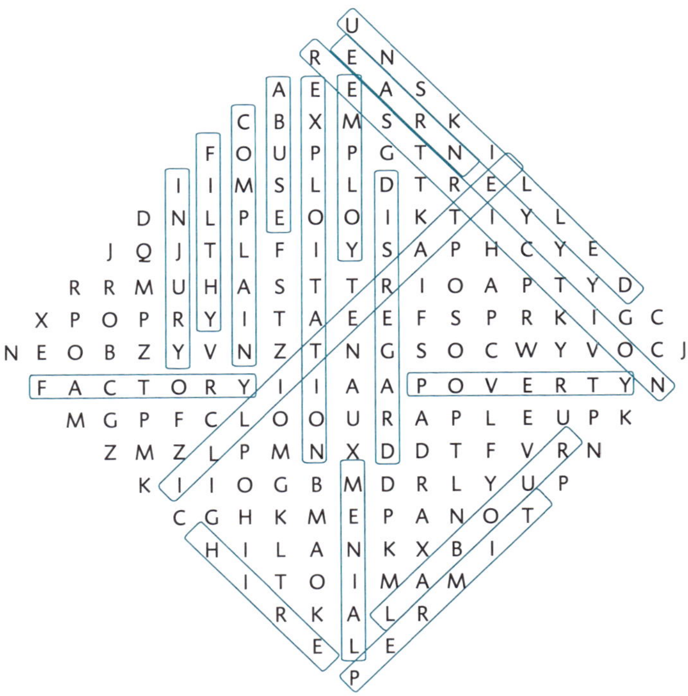

78

A) publisher
B) gather
C) source
D) drought
E) embrace
F) presume
G) stamina
H) jungle
G) population

79

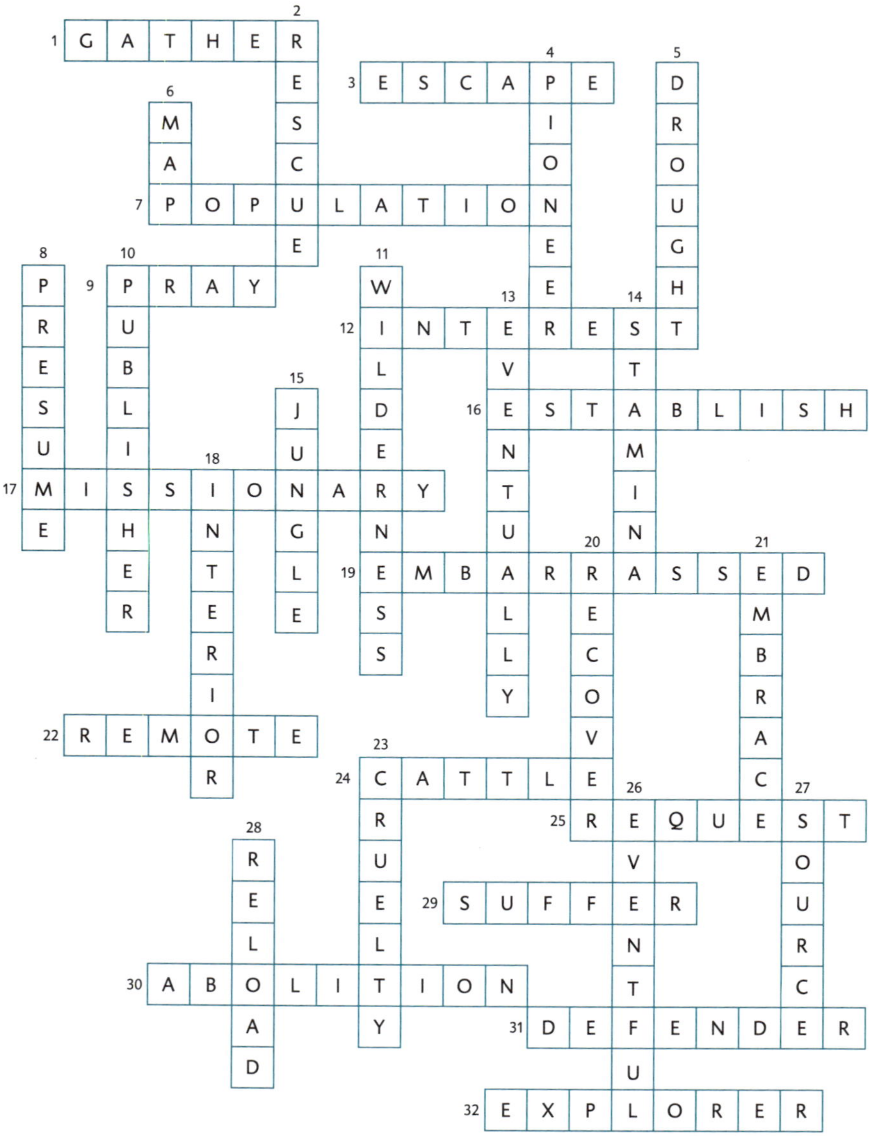

How to paraphrase

80 a)
- youngsters = teenagers, children
- delinquents = young/juvenile offenders
- entertaining = amusing, enjoyable, fun
- depressing = saddening
- homes = families

b)
- criminologist = a person who studies crime and criminals
- to play truant = to stay away from school

81

Word	Order	Paraphrase
stupid	2	1 to say one will do harm if a person does not do what is desired
divorce	4	2 opposite of intelligent, clever
gossip	5	3 the good and evil that happens to people; great wealth
deprive	7	4 legal separation of husband and wife by court of law
threaten	1	5 useless talk, usually about other people and their mistakes
fortune	3	6 causing anger; insulting and disgusting
offensive	6	7 to take away from sb

Word formation: prefixes and suffixes

82

advantage	disadvantage	decision	indecision
ability	inability, disability	honour	dishonour
appearance	disappearance	literacy	illiteracy
balance	imbalance	patience	impatience

83

agree	disagree	do	undo
appear	disappear	like	dislike
believe	disbelieve	plug	unplug
connect	disconnect	understand	misunderstand

84

convenient	inconvenient	educated	uneducated
able	unable	happy	unhappy
breakable	unbreakable	legal	illegal
dependent	independent	pleasant	unpleasant

85

certain	certainty	free	freedom
employ	employment	pay	payment
enter	entrance	real	reality
foolish	foolishness	sick	sickness

86

act	active	forget	forgetful
centre	central	noise	noisy
comic	comical	poison	poisonous
courage	courageous	read	readable
fashion	fashionable	use	useful

Combinations and collocations

87
a) The film *Mutiny on the Bounty* **brought** fame to the actors Charles Laughton and Clark Gable.
b) We are having a party on Saturday. Please come and **bring** your girlfriend Eve, too.
c) I'm sorry about your headache. Let's finish our meal and then I'll **take** you home.
d) Robbie, please **bring** me the coat you wore at the playground. Let me check if it has to be **taken** to the cleaner's.
f) As it was getting rather late, my father **took** Anne and Robert to the station in his car.
f) John visited me in hospital and **brought** me some lovely flowers.
g) Our history teacher is **taking** us on a trip to Rome next month.

88

A	B	C	D	E	F	G
5	1	7	2	3	4	6

89 John Red Cloud Walcott is a Native American activist. He works towards improving the situation of Native Americans in the reservations. In 1992, in his speech to commemorate the 500th anniversary of the landing of Columbus on American soil, he said: "Even the US President admits that there is too **much** poverty among the Native Americans. But why doesn't anyone do anything?

We all know what happened in the past. There have been **lots of (a lot of/ plenty of)** TV reports about the cruel treatment of American Indians by the pioneers. **A lot of (Lots of/Plenty of)** people know that the arrival of the Europeans did not do the Indians **much** good! For so **many** years they have been neglected. How **much** longer do they have to wait for better opportunities? Why don't they receive as **much** support as other ethnic minorities? Is it because there aren't too **many** of us left to have political influence? Most politicians do **a lot of (lots of/plenty of)** talking but don't offer **much** help. There aren't **many** Native American families who live comfortable and wealthy lives. Native Americans have **a lot of (lots of/plenty of)** trouble when they try to find a job. How **many** employers prefer a coloured applicant to a white jobseeker?"

90
a) I'm terribly thirsty – I must **have a drink** right away!
b) Dad isn't pleased with your coming home so late every night. He wants to **have a talk** to you.
c) Shirley, you have worked very hard these last few hours; **have a rest**!
d) We don't have to do all this work ourselves, boss. I'll **have it done** for us.
e) My nose keeps running; I think I **have a cold**.
f) Anne and Robert have been married for eight years and they have never gone abroad in the summer. But this year they'll **have a holiday** in France.
g) You went to the disco last night, didn't you? Did you **have fun**?

91

do	make	take
one's best	the best of sth	a break
a course	an effort	a course
one's hair	a film	an exam
one's (home)work	a mistake	notes
	a noise	a photo(graph)
	an offer	

92
a) The fridge is almost empty! Before we start cooking, we need to **do the shopping** first.
b) My sister spends three hours in front of the mirror to **do her hair**.

c) That was a tasty meal, Jim. But now I feel really tired. Could you help me **do the dishes**, please?
d) You've worked so hard. I hope you **do well** in your exam.
e) The Taylors seem to have loads of money. Do you happen to know what Mr. Taylor **does for a living**?
f) Greg, before you leave for school: Have you **done your homework** for today?

False friends

93 a) Thousands of poor Cuban migrants try to sail across the **sea** to America.
b) The Everglades once covered the entire tip of Florida – about 4 million acres of wetland stretching from **Lake** Okeechobee in the north to the Gulf of Mexico in the south.
c) Lois cries, "Superman, if you can **hear** me, drop what you're doing and help me!"
d) British generals proposed a military land, **sea** and air blockade to fight the dictatorial regime.
e) Our teacher never has time **listen to** the worries and concerns of his students.
f) Scientists suspect that pesticides and other toxic chemicals are discharged into rivers and out to **sea**, killing marine life.
g) Lots of immigrants would be **happy** to work for money or food.
h) Billy Graham would practise sermons aloud in old sheds or in a canoe in the middle of a **lake**.
i) Nelson Mandela only used violence when the other side would not **listen**.
j) After the shooting, the criminal threw the gun into a **lake**.
k) Did you **hear** the story of the tourist who got lost in the maze at Hampton Court?

94 The early death of Lord Carnarvon, sponsor of Howard Carter, **became** the starting point of a legend: that of "the curse of the pharaoh". Shortly after its discovery in 1922, the tomb of the pharaoh had **obtained** the status of a world sensation. Millions of readers wanted to know everything about the **current** state of the excavations. Thousands of visitors **eventually/actually** travelled to Egypt to have a look at the site themselves. **Eventually** a journalist got so bored with ordinary reports on the diggings that when yet another member of Carter's crew – Archibald Reid – died, he invented a sensational headline: "Has Reid **become** another victim of the curse of Tutankhamen?" A new "mystery" was created: Everyone who had taken part in the opening of the tomb would not **become** old. The ghost of the dead pharaoh would **eventually** cause his early death. That was the punishment for those who had **obtained** access to the burial chamber. In the 1930s the general public had **become** so interested in the mysterious deaths that Hollywood producers **eventually/actually** made films on the subject. The film *The Mummy* (1932), for example, was to **become** a horror classic. Today we know that all 20 people in Carter's crew **actually** died natural deaths: due to infections, illnesses or even suicide. The mysterious deaths have thus been explained, but the Valley of Kings has **perhaps** more secrets in store.

95 Few people would say that Marilyn Monroe's acting was **excellent**, but according to the **opinion** of actors who played in films alongside her, she was a **sensitive** creature. It is true, though, that she was hard to work with.
Most of all, her extravagancy was due to the cruel treatment she had received from **unscrupulous** photographers and managers since she first started as a starlet and pin-up girl. She was born on June 1, 1926 as Norma Jean Baker, an illegitimate child who never knew her father. Growing up in poverty and misery didn't help her to develop any **self-confidence**. A 21-year-old aircraft plant worker **became** her hero and rescued her from that dreadful background. Norma Jean married him when she was 16 and began working as a model for bathing costumes. In order to **become/get** famous and earn more money she also started posing for pin-ups and glamour photos. A Hollywood producer saw her photos, offered her a contract and renamed her Marilyn Monroe.
At first she was only given smaller roles because of the stiff **competition** in the film industry, but eventually she played in major films, usually taking the role of the dumb blonde. Millions liked to see her that way and queued in front of the cinemas to buy **tickets** for her latest film.
On August 5, 1962, she committed suicide by taking an overdose of sleeping pills, worried about getting old and losing her sex appeal. She had always relied on other people's **opinion** too much. She had never found her own role in life, had always acted a part.

Linkers

96 What the Spaniards and the other conquerors did to the native population and their culture has not been forgotten. The 500th anniversary of the explorers' first landing on American shores (1992) had been planned as a great celebration. **However**, Columbus Day, October 12, became a day of protest. Native Americans and other groups staged big demonstrations **because** they wanted to remind the world of the genocide of their people. **That means** they see the arrival of Columbus and his successors as the tragic beginning of the extinction of many indigenous peoples of America.

To the soldiers and settlers of the westward movement the Indians were wild, stupid creatures. **However**, words like those of Indian Chief Seattle prove that the Indians really knew better: "We know that the white man does not understand our ways. One portion of land is the same to him as the next, **for** he is a stranger who comes in the night and takes from the land whatever he needs. The earth is not his brother, **but** his enemy, and **when** he has conquered it, he moves on." Today, the two million American Indians form one of the smallest ethnic groups in the United States. **As a result** they have hardly any influence on modern American society. **Unless** all of us support the just cause of the Native Americans, their life in the reservations will still be characterised by extreme poverty, mass unemployment, alcoholism and teenage suicide.

97
a) **To begin with**, at the end of the 15th century, there were still about 100 million Native Americans.
b) **Whereas** the Mayas and Aztecs lived in the territory that is now Mexico, the Incas had settled in western South America, including modern Peru and parts of Ecuador, Chile and Argentina.
c) **As a result of** the arrival of the European settlers, the life of the Native Americans changed for the worse and their number declined dramatically.
d) Just two hundred years after Columbus set foot on the Bahamas, **for example**, there were only four million natives left.
e) **Because** the European settlers drove native people away into the less fertile areas, the Native Americans were robbed of their land.
f) **Moreover**, many Native Americans died of infectious diseases, such as measles, brought by the Europeans.
g) **In addition**, a lot of Natives Americans did not survive the cruel treatment they suffered as slaves or were killed by the settlers who used firearms against them in battles.

Writing

An email about what really matters to young Australians

98 a)
- **Young Australians' concerns:** stress, school and body image
- **Important matters:** alcohol and drugs, equity and discrimination, economy and financial matters
- **Differences between female and male teenagers' attitudes:** female teenagers are more concerned about their academic achievements than their male counterparts; young women are also more worried that they might not have the money to achieve their aims

b) *Sample solution:*

Hi Jamie

Thanks for your e-mail and for sending the results of the Mission Australia survey. Taking part in it must have been pretty exciting! I was surprised that young Australians claimed alcohol and drugs were their top issue. Smoking and binge drinking are considered increasingly uncool amongst teenagers in Germany. I guess school-related stress would have been my priority. Everybody in my class is aware that good qualifications are essential in finding a training position or regularly paid work. This makes life rather stressful for many pupils. Parents often don't help – they increase the pressure with their high expectations.

It is no surprise to me that girls seem to worry much more about their academic potential or financial security than boys do. I believe most people who indicated that their body image was a major concern were also female. I don't think there are big differences between Australians and Germans.

Still, the survey indicates that in spite of their concerns about education more than fifty per cent of young Australians look to the future with confidence. I think the majority of my friends share this optimistic view.

What puzzles me a bit is that the survey does not say much about young people's interest in politics. In Germany, the number of teenagers who care about climate change, immigration or xenophobia is increasing steadily.

But what about you? Do you feel well represented in this survey or are you rather disappointed by the results? Write back soon!

Best
Noah

(253 words)

A letter to deal with the chocolate crisis

99 a) • **Pay attention to the issue the customer addresses:** We are very sorry to hear that our product has given reason for complaint. Keeping our customers satisfied has always been our top priority.
- **Give plausible reasons:** The product might not have been stored properly. The box has probably been exposed to humidity.
- **Offer compensation:** We apologise and offer a refund. Please provide us with your bank account details in order for us to reimburse you.

b) *Sample solution:*

Lawson's Chocolate Factory
TERRY LAWSON & SONS LIMITED
35 AUDEN TERRACE
YORK, YO2 5YE

Ms Mary Jane Smith
5 Filmer Road
Fulham
London SW6 7JE

30th July, 20 ...

Dear Ms Smith

Thank you for your letter. We are very sorry you have recently been disappointed by the condition in which you have found our confectionery.

We regret, however, that you did not send in the product for examination so we are unable to ascertain the cause of the fault. From your letter, we suspect that this confectionery has been affected by unsatisfactory handling or storage conditions.

We hope that you will accept and enjoy the fresh Lawson's Premium Collection which we are sending to you, together with our apologies for the disappointment and inconvenience caused.

Yours sincerely

E. Schmiedinger

Ella Schmiedinger,
Consumer Service Department

(100 words)

A blog entry on crossing the Alps in 7 days

100 a) **A:** Made it! The first member of our group has reached the summit and is rewarded by a magnificent view from the top.

B: Hiking is fun, but long backpacking trips can cause foot pain and blisters.

C: An open air kitchen. The chef is about to prepare a healthy, nutritious meal for a hungry crowd in no time.

D: All packed up and ready for our next day's adventure.

b) *Sample solution:*

Hello everybody

Here comes news from our tour across the Alps in seven days. There is so much to see and do on our hiking tour through Bavaria and Tyrol that there doesn't seem to be enough time for taking photographs and writing long posts. So here are a few snapshots and a quick note to let you know we are all fine and enjoying a wonderful adventure.
We started off along the coastline of Lake Tegernsee to get used to hiking. It was a pleasant start walking through lovely scenery. We were all in good shape and finally ready for the more challenging stages. One result of the steeper and more exhausting trips on the two following days can be seen on Bill's left foot: two giant blisters. Otherwise everybody was fine, thanks to Janet and Harry, who conjured up the most amazing meals from almost nothing.
Today we crossed the Alpine Main Ridge. Despite the blisters, Bill was the first to reach the first summit. It was a challenging walk and we were all happy to put up our tents in the evening. However, after a good night's sleep we will be confident and fit again. Watch this blog to see how we are getting on.

P. S. Next summer, we will walk from Fort William (Scotland) to the summit of Ben Nevis, the highest mountain in Britain. Drop us a line if you're interested in joining our rambling group (for e-mail contact see address below). All hiking enthusiasts are welcome. *(253 words)*

A letter to the editor on extreme advertising

101 a) The picture shows a young black boy placed in the middle of a giant supermarket trolley. The child, who may be between 4 and 6 years of age, is holding out his two empty hands, begging for food. The boy has an anxious expression on his face. In the bottom right-hand corner of the photo one can see the forearm of a white person handing a tin of beans to the boy. On the handle of the trolley, there is a message for the shopper: "See how easy feeding the hungry can be?" *(93 words)*

b) The message of the picture is a plea to do something to combat starvation. Hunger is still a widespread problem in many emerging nations and children are especially affected. Their physical and mental health is endangered if they are undernourished. The photo collage of the child in the shopping trolley is rather shocking, but it captures people's attention and (hopefully) makes them aware of the misery of poor and starving children – perhaps more than words in a newspaper article.

c) *Sample solution:*

Dear Sir or Madam

Returning from a holiday in South Africa I read your article "Feed SA is far beyond the pale" condemning the NGO's latest advertising campaign against world hunger. I do not agree with your criticism and would like to tell you why.

Thousands of reports have been shown on TV, and thousands of articles have been written in newspapers and magazines about malnutrition and starvation in many parts of the developing world. So everybody should know about the problem.

However, what has been done about it? Not much or not enough, as I sadly experienced during my recent holiday. In the townships I saw many poor blacks still struggling to feed themselves and their families. It is a disgrace that middle-class people throw away food every day while millions are dying of hunger.

In my view, words and news reports alone don't get the message through to people to motivate them to do something. This is why we need more drastic methods. This is why we need disturbing campaigns such as the one started by Feed SA. A supermarket is the right place for this campaign as this is where people buy their own food and might be able to afford smaller donations for Feed SA as well, in the form of canned goods, for example.

I strongly recommend you reconsider your attitude towards this honest, innovative and straightforward approach that will help to eradicate starvation.

Yours faithfully

Hannah Berger *(243 words)*

A cartoon analysis on environmental issues

102 a)

Above the water	Under the water
• a Greenpeace boat and a fishing boat in the top left-hand corner • a huge black cloud of smoke coming from the chimney of the fishing boat • a speech bubble over the fishing trawler saying, "Oh no! Not that Greenpeace ship again! Those guys only cause trouble!"	• a huge fishing net dragged along by the fishing boat • one single fish, labelled the "last blue tuna", about to swim into the enormous empty net • the tuna seeming unsure about what he sees in front of him

b) *Sample solution:*

The cartoonist is criticising the extinction of fish species and the destruction of marine life. The huge drag net symbolises the industrial fishing methods which are employed worldwide to exploit the resources of our oceans. The cartoonist uses the example of the blue tuna to illustrate the fact that overfishing threatens the survival of many species. The real culprits in the disaster – the floating fish factories – want to divert the public's attention away from their destructive practices by denouncing Greenpeace activists, who warn of the fatal consequences, as troublemakers. The cartoon can also be seen as a general warning concerning man's ruthless exploitation of resources, which will eventually result in the disappearance of not only fish, but also mammals, like the Siberian tiger, or insects such as butterflies. *(128 words)*

An analysis of statistics on teenage pregnancies

103 a)

Year	England (development)	Wales (development)
1998	47 per thousand (increase since 1997)	55 per thousand (considerable increase since 1997)
2001	42 per thousand (slight decrease since 1998)	45 per thousand (significant decrease since 1998)
2006	41 per thousand (relatively stable since 2001)	43 per thousand (relatively stable since 2001)
2013	25 per thousand (remarkable decrease since 2007)	28 per thousand (remarkable decrease since 2008)

b) *Sample solution:*

The graph illustrates the number of teenagers (women aged 15 to 17) in England and Wales who conceived a child between 1993 and 2013. There are two lines which represent the conception rates in each of these countries. The figure shows that conception rates of women younger than 18 years of age have fallen significantly over the measured 20 years, i. e. by almost 50 per cent. While 47 teenagers per thousand conceived in England in 1998, only 24 per thousand did so in 2013. In comparison, numbers in Wales are slightly higher, at 55 per thousand in 1998 and 28 per thousand in 2013, but suggest the same trend. The year-on-year decline began in 1998, with both countries reaching their lowest levels ever in 2013. The drop in underage conceptions in England and Wales was particularly sharp between 2007 and 2013: teenage pregnancies decreased from 41 to 25 per thousand in England and 44 to 28 per thousand in Wales. *(161 words)*

A report on media usage

104 a)

Level of necessity	Boys 5–7	Boys 8–11	Boys 12–15	Girls 5–7	Girls 8–11	Girls 12–15
most important	TV (58 %)	TV (30 %)	mobile (29 %)	TV (52 %)	TV (38 %)	mobile (46 %)
fairly important (name 2)	games (15 %), tablet (13 %)	games (22 %), tablet (15 %)	games (22 %), TV (18 %)	tablet (17 %), books (14 %)	tablet (18 %), books (14 %)	TV (18 %), tablet (16 %)
least important	MP3, radio, DVD / Blu-ray player					

b) *Sample solution:*

In 2014, British boys and girls aged 5 to 15 were asked, "Which one of the things you use almost every day would you miss the most if it weren't there anymore?" The bar chart illustrates the results of the survey.
TV took first place in the list of most missed devices among children up to the age of 11. In particular, it was the preferred medium for more than half of the youngest age group (5-7). When children reached their teenage years, mobile phones became their favourite device. In comparison, young people between 12 and 15 years of age would not have missed a television that much. It is remarkable that in this age bracket, girls showed a greater preference for mobile phones than boys. Almost half of them (46 per cent) would have missed their mobile most compared to about a third of the boys (29 per cent). In addition, more girls than boys aged 12 to 15 would have missed a tablet computer (16 per cent as opposed to 9 per cent). It is not surprising that in each age group more boys than girls would have missed a games console or player most. Between 5 and 11 years of age, boys preferred playing games whereas girls showed greater interest in books, magazines and comics. Irrespective of gender and age, the MP3 players, DVD and Blu-ray players and the radio were the devices least missed. *(239 words)*

An application for a summer job

105 a) **main requirements:**

- minimum age 16
- monitoring safety and assisting guests

- ability to complete lifeguard training programme
- assistance in cleaning park area and facilities

benefits:

- lifeguard training paid for
- payment of $ 15.00 an hour for approximately 35 hours a week
- free lodging
- prospect of future employment

b)

To... alistair.paull@starfish-waterpark.com

Cc...

Subject: Summer job lifeguard Lukas Neumann

Dear Mr Paull

I am writing to express my interest in the summer job of a lifeguard at Starfish Waterpark, as advertised on your website.

I am 17 years old, and at the moment I am attending a "Wirtschaftsgymnasium" (Commercial College of Further Education), from which I will graduate next year. My plans for the future are to study business administration at a university and later work in the running of a theme park – here in Germany or abroad.

Being a swimming enthusiast I have been a member of the "Deutsche Lebens-Rettungs-Gesellschaft" (DLRG, the German Life Saving Association) since I was ten. I attended special courses to acquire knowledge and skills in water safety. I hold several certificates, among them the "Deutsches Rettungsschwimm-abzeichen Silber" (German lifeguard award, silver).

I am anxious to improve my water safety management skills at a waterpark abroad. Completing the lifeguard training programme which you offer would be of tremendous help.

My knowledge of foreign languages includes German (native speaker) and a good working knowledge of English and French. My interests, apart from swimming, are music, travelling and the protection of the environment (I am the co-founder of the Environmental Kids Club in my hometown).

I would very much like to be given the opportunity to work in your renowned water park (this summer and summers to come) and look forward to hearing from you soon.

Yours sincerely

Lukas Neumann

(234 words)

A comment on boarding schools

106 a) Arguments **in favour** of Monboit's view:

- sending children to boarding school at an early age scars them for life
- boarding schools are outdated institutions
- boarding schools are expensive institutions that only an elite can afford

Arguments **against** Monboit's view:

- parents send their children to boarding schools because the education provided there is said to be better than at state schools
- the comment is exaggerated and biased: not all boarders become unfeeling or emotionally disabled individuals
- boarding (i. e. being away from home at an early age) helps children become independent and self-reliant

b) *Sample solution:*

In a comment on *The Guardian's* website, the journalist George Monboit criticises the disastrous effect boarding schools can have on the character and emotional development of young children.

Monboit argues that separating children from their parents at such an early age is cruel. The biographies of famous boarding school students prove his point: Both George Orwell and Winston Churchill, for example, hated their days at their public schools. However, it is widely exaggerated to claim that all boarders are emotionally unstable and do not care for the feelings of others. Going away to school can also teach them to be independent and self-reliant.

It has to be said that in a modern society boarding schools are not the only option to provide a child with a good education. There are a large number of public schools that do not require children to stay overnight on the school premises. However, the general problem remains: privately-run schools cost a great deal of money. So, most parents are not able to afford to send their children there. Unfortunately, it seems that public school education opens up better career opportunities to pupils. The reason is simple. As tutor groups are smaller, pupils receive a better education. This is why public school students achieve far better results in final exams than state school students.

However, I think Monboit misses the most important point. He should use his influence as a journalist to make the government invest more money in state schools to bring them up to the standard of public schools. *(256 words)*

Bildnachweis

S. 1: © Dudarev Mikhail. Shutterstock
S. 2: **Icon** (all chapters) © mostafa fawzy/fotolia.com; **Newspaper** © Feng Yu. Shutterstock
S. 7–9: **Cobain** © Frank Micelotta/Getty Images; **Jackson** © Zoran Veselinovic, licensed under CC BY-SA 2.0; **Winehouse** © Rama, licensed under CC BY-SA 2.0 FR
S. 11: Tdoes1/dreamstime.com
S. 13: nasirkhan. Shutterstock
S. 15: **Boy** © Djomas. Shutterstock; **Girl** © Skydive.Erick. Shutterstock
S. 19: **A** © DOPhoto. Shutterstock; **B** © Viktor Gladkov. Shutterstock; **C** © Nejron Photo. Shutterstock; **D** © 123rf.com; **E** © Kzenon. Shutterstock; **F** © oliveromg. Shutterstock
S. 20: © Ashwin. Shutterstock
S. 25, 155: **High heels** © Photobac. Shutterstock; **Slippers** © zhekoss. Shutterstock
S. 26: © Goodluz. Shutterstock
S. 27: **A** © Gareth Boden. Pearson Education Ltd; **B**, **C** © Monkey Business Images. Shutterstock; **D** © Elaine Willcock. Shutterstock
S. 31: © Jon Barlow. Pearson Education Ltd
S. 32: © Rob Byron. Shutterstock
S. 34: © UK Home Office [CC BY 2.0 (http://creativecommons.org/licenses/by/2.0)], via Wikimedia
S. 35: © Prime Minister's Office, 10 Downing Street, licensed under the Open Government Licence v1.0
S. 35/36, 163/164: **Teenager in car** © Lisa Turay. Shutterstock; **College class** © Robert Kneschke. Shutterstock; **Mosque** © Ann Cromack. Ikat Design. Pearson Education Ltd; **Bride and groom** © Blend Images. Shutterstock; **Waitress** © Wavebreak Premium. Shutterstock; **Block of flats** © c0llinsphoto. Shutterstock
S. 37: © Cheuk-king Lo. Pearson Education Asia Ltd
S. 39: © Jules Selmes. Pearson Education Ltd
S. 40: © Andresr. Shutterstock
S. 41: © Lifdiz. Shutterstock
S. 42: © Robert Kneschke. Shutterstock
S. 45: © Studio 8. Pearson Education Ltd
S. 47: © Bn Campos. Shutterstock
S. 50: © Sandra Caldwell. Shutterstock
S. 55: © Maksym Gorpenyuk. Shutterstock
S. 59: © Pedro Bento. Shutterstock
S. 66: © Can Stock Photo Inc./sumners
S. 71: © Rido. Shutterstock
S. 75: Ham II, licensed under CC BY-SA 3.0
S. 79: © Christopher Bowers/dreamstime.com
S. 81: Allstar Picture Library/MGM
S. 83: © Scott Rothstein. Shutterstock
S. 85: © Roberto Caucino. Shutterstock
S. 87: © Maximus256. Shutterstock
S. 89/90: © iurii. Shutterstock
S. 92/93: **A** © pzAxe. Shutterstock; **B** © bikeriderlondon. Shutterstock; **C** © Joseph C. Salonis. Shutterstock; **D** © irabel8. Shutterstock; **E** © 123rf.com; **F** © Monkey Business Images. Shutterstock
S. 96/97: © Alexander Raths. Shutterstock
S. 100: © Ljupco Smokovski. Shutterstock
S. 101: © Mike Flippo. Shutterstock
S. 103: © KKulikov. Shutterstock
S. 105: © EBFoto. Shutterstock
S. 107: © Tracy Whiteside. Shutterstock
S. 115: © Rido. Shutterstock
S. 122, 147: © 123rf.com
S. 125: © Steve Cadman, licensed under CC BY-SA 2.0
S. 126: © Harry Burton/The New York Times 1922
S. 127: © Can Stock Photo Inc./labamba
S. 130: © VICTOR TORRES. Shutterstock
S. 131: © Dragon Images. Shutterstock
S. 136: **A** © oksix. Shutterstock; **B** © Patrick Poendl/dreamstime.com; **C** © Trevor Clifford. Pearson Education Ltd; **D** © Tyler Olson. Shutterstock
S. 143/144: **Mouse** © Graham Briggs – www.sxc.hu; **lifebelt** © Iaroslav Neliubov. Shutterstock
S. 145: © Snap2Art. Shutterstock